7/98

10
—
1

12/8

198

HENRY MOORE

David Mitchinson y Julian Stallabrass

HENRY MOORE

EDICIONES POLÍGRAFA, S. A.

© *1992 Ediciones Polígrafa, S. A.*
Balmes, 54 - 08007 BARCELONA (Spain)

Text copyright © David Mitchinson and Julian Stallabrass
Photographs copyright © The Henry Moore Foundation

ISBN 84-343-0672-7
Dep. Legal: B. 1.473 - 1992 (Printed in Spain)

Color separations by Reprocolor Llovet, S. A., Barcelona
Printed and bound by La Polígrafa, S. A.
Parets del Vallès (Barcelona)

CONTENTS

HENRY MOORE: THE EARLY YEARS

David Mitchinson

At the turn of the century Castleford, West Yorkshire, was a small industrial town, with coalmining its main activity. It was in no way picturesque, but was within easy reach of some fine countryside and attractive villages. It was here that Henry Moore was born, on 30 July 1898, and here that he spent his childhood.

During his second year at Castleford Secondary School there arrived a new, young art teacher who would remain Moore's friend and mentor throughout his formative years. Alice Gostick had a French mother with whom she lived, and her interests stretched far beyond the provincial backwater of West Yorkshire. She was aware of all the artistic developments taking place in Europe: news of Post-Impressionism, the Vienna Secession and Art Nouveau reached her young pupils.

Moore passed the Cambridge Senior Certificate when he was sixteen. He was determined to sit the examinations for a scholarship to the local art college, but his father, ever a practical man, thought that he should follow an elder sister into the teaching profession. After a brief introduction as student teacher, Moore began working full-time at his old school in Castleford. He was also asked, as an older boy, to design and carve a Roll of Honour for the names of all the former students who were marching off to war. Soon it was to be his turn; he enlisted at the age of eighteen and presently joined the 15th Battalion The London Regiment, known as the Civil Service Rifles.

Despite the heavy training schedules, Moore found time to make his first visits to the British Museum and the National Gallery in London. But soon he was sent to France, where he and his regiment participated in what should have been the last great battle of the war, Cambrai. For Moore, active participation in the war ceased when, along with many of his comrades, he was gassed. He was able to walk ten miles to a field hospital before his condition deteriorated and he was sent back to England. After convalescence he became a physical training instructor and later returned to France, but by then the war was over. Moore went back to his teaching post in Castleford, but he now knew that teaching in school was not for him. He applied for and received an ex-serviceman's grant to attend Leeds School of Art. There was no sculpture tutor at Leeds, but because Moore insisted that he wanted to study sculpture, one was appointed. At the end of his second year he won a scholarship to the Royal College of Art in London.

Now followed a period of intense activity for Moore, a thirsting for knowledge, an outpouring of ideas, many of them into the pages of notebooks which have survived to this day. There are five extant hard-backed notebooks dated between

Henry Moore at the marble quarries near Querceta in the Carrara mountains

7

1922 and 1926 and evidence of the existence of another two. In 1928 came the Underground Relief Notebook, the first entirely devoted to drawings for sculpture, including *West Wind* 1928–9 [LH 58] and *Reclining Figure* [fig. 1]. Thereafter the notebooks become sketchbooks, containing hundreds of sketches showing the original ideas from which the sculptures were to develop. Moore studied and drew the collections in the Victoria and Albert Museum and the Tate Gallery, but his greatest interest lay in the British Museum, where he examined intently the collection of Mexican Aztec sculpture. He called this activity 'museuming'. He read Roger Fry and Henry Gaudier-Brzeska, became acquainted with the work of Jacob Epstein, and visited Paris for the first time in 1923. In 1924 Moore won a travelling scholarship to Europe, but he postponed going for a year in order to accept an appointment as sculpture instructor at the Royal College.

In 1928 he met Irina Radetsky, a painting student at the college. They were married the following year and settled in London at 11A Parkhill Road, Hampstead. This consisted of a small studio on the ground floor and an equally small flat above. Off a side street facing Parkhill Road ran an alleyway with a series of eight ateliers, known as the Mall Studios. When the Moores arrived, No. 7 was the home of the sculptors John Skeaping and his wife Barbara Hepworth.

Hampstead was the hub of creativity in London during the thirties and the Moores quickly made friends among the other artists, writers and architects in the district. During the decade many notable figures moved within a radius of about a mile, including Marcel Breuer, Wells Coates and Walter Gropius, Ivon Hitchens, E. L. T. Mesens, Piet Mondrian, Paul Nash, Ben Nicholson, Roland Penrose and Adrian Stokes. The whole area became more international as the decade progressed, due to the arrival of refugees from the Continent.

The head of the Sculpture Department at the Victoria and Albert Museum, Richard Bedford, who was very interested in direct carving, had a cottage on the East Anglian coast near Sizewell, where the Moores, Skeaping, Hepworth and others would go for holidays. Moore brought back ironstone pebbles which he turned into small carvings. He also found chalk pebbles under Shakespeare Cliff in Kent and these too he used for carvings. He studied the native British

Fig. 1
Reclining Figure, 1929 [LH 59]
Brown Hornton stone, L 83.8 cm

stones in the Geological Museum in London and visited quarries in different parts of the country looking for suitable material. Skeaping discovered Cumberland alabaster and Moore bought a few blocks which were sent down to London. He also had Hopton Wood stone sent from Derbyshire and both green and brown Hornton stone from Edgehill.

Throughout the decade Moore was carving between seven and twenty works a year, and the small studio was soon crowded with finished sculptures and work in progress. The largest work he carved at Parkhill Road was the *Reclining Woman* [fig. 2], now in Ottawa at the National Gallery of Canada. This piece, just under a metre long, would seem quite small by today's standards but at the time Moore had tremendous problems getting the block of stone into the studio. This lack of working space which, combined with difficulty of access, made working on a larger scale impossible forced Moore to look for somewhere in the country with plenty of room. Using a small legacy of Irina's, the couple bought a cottage at Barfreston in Kent in 1931, and then in 1934 moved to a house called Burcroft in Kingston, a few miles away. This had five acres of land, which gave Moore all the space he needed. The blocks of Hopton Wood stone which had come down from Derbyshire were erected in the garden, and seeing them in the landscape gave Moore fresh ideas for sculpture.

Moore had exhibited three sculptures in a mixed exhibition at the Redfern Gallery, London, in the spring of 1924. These were *Head* in terracotta, *Dancing Figure* in bronze and *Carving* in marble.[1] His first one-man exhibition, which consisted of 42 sculptures and 51 drawings, was at the Warren Gallery, London, in 1928. Among the buyers were Augustus John, Henry Lamb and Jacob Epstein.

His second exhibition, this time consisting of 34 sculptures and 19 drawings, was held at the Leicester Galleries in 1931. Epstein wrote in the catalogue foreword: 'What is so clearly expressed is a vision rich in sculptural invention, avoiding the banalities of abstraction and concentrating upon those enduring elements that constitute great sculpture... sculpture in England is without imagination or direction. Here in Henry Moore's work are both qualities.' From this exhibition came the first sale to a gallery abroad: a small *Head* in ironstone, which was purchased by Dr Max Sauerlandt, the director of the Museum für Kunst und Gewerbe in Hamburg (later destroyed). Not all the response was

Fig. 2
Reclining Woman, 1930 [LH 84]
Green Hornton stone, L 94 cm

favourable, however. The art critic of the London *Morning Post* led the opposition with: 'The cult of ugliness triumphs at the hands of Mr Moore. He shows an utter contempt for the natural beauty of women and children, and in doing so, deprives even stone of its value as a means of aesthetic and emotional expression', and, 'Aesthetic detachment is bound to atrophy soul and vision and lead to revolting formlessness such as offends sensitive people.'

At the Royal College these attacks were taken up by Moore's immediate superior, who wanted him removed to make way for a favourite of his own, and by the ex-students' association which called for his dismissal. Though supported by the principal Sir William Rothenstein, Moore decided to move on and declined to renew his contract at the Royal College. He went instead to Chelsea School of Art, where he restarted the sculpture school and then taught for two days a week until 1940.

Throughout the twenties Moore was drawing from life: 'life drawing had been a continual struggle to understand the complete three-dimensional form of the model and to express it on the flat surface of the paper'.[2] But by 1932 he was becoming less preoccupied with life drawing, though it continued in his work in decreasing amounts until 1935. He was no longer studying the collections at the British Museum but had turned towards the observation of nature, an interest which stayed with him all his life. He studied natural forms first in the Natural History Museum in London, and later began his famous collection of 'found objects'. He described some of the natural forms as follows:

> Pebbles and rocks show Nature's way of working stone. Smooth, sea-
> worn pebbles show the wearing away, rubbed treatment of stone
> and principles of asymmetry. Rocks show the hacked, hewn treatment
> of stone, and have a jagged nervous block rhythm. Bones have
> marvellous structural strength and hard tenseness of form, subtle
> transition of one shape into the next and great variety in section.
> Trees (tree trunks) show principles of growth and strength of joints,
> with easy passing of one section into the next... Shells show nature's
> hard but hollow form (metal sculpture) and have a wonderful
> completeness of single shape.[3]

The drawings of these years, now known as the 'transformation drawings', begin with studies of closely observed small natural forms — a piece of stone, a lobster claw, shells, twigs, bones, pebbles — dozens of sketches showing these objects from every possible view. Slowly, while drawing, the objects begin to change,

Fig. 3
Transformation Drawing: Ideas for Sculpture, 1930 [HMF 808]
Pencil, brush and ink, 200 × 238 mm

Fig. 4
Mother and Child, 1932 [LH 121]
Green Hornton stone, H 88.9 cm

or be transformed, into recognisable and realisable sculptural forms. A bone becomes a reclining figure, a shell a half figure, a stone a head and shoulders. During this period almost all Moore's carvings can be related to these transformation drawings. *Composition* 1931 [plate 17] can be seen to have evolved from a bone form in the sketches on the right-hand side of a drawing [fig. 3]. From 1933–4 onwards came a succession of sketchbook pages full of 'Ideas for Sculpture', 'Ideas for Several Piece compositions', 'Square Forms' and 'Ideas for wood sculpture' corresponding to most of the carvings.[4]

Mother and Child [fig. 4] is the most ambitious of the larger stone carvings of the early 1930s. It seems from contemporary photographic evidence that Moore may have intended making the mother a draped figure, with folds of drapery covering the lower portion of the body from the knees to the feet. This may account for the somewhat unresolved solution at the base, where the feet and calves appear disproportionately large to enable them to become part of the structure of the seat.[5] This apart, Moore has produced a tremendous balance between the various angularities of the figure. Besides looking back to the Pre-Columbian influence, particularly in the treatment of the head, the confident position of this head and the thrusting line of the shoulders make the sculpture a forerunner of the *Reclining Mother and Child* of 1975–6 [plates 151, 152]. Between 1930 and 1932 Moore carved a total of twelve Mother and Child sculptures. However, after 1932 there were no new developments of the figurative mother and child theme until the terracotta figures made at the end of the war as preliminary studies for the carving *Madonna and Child* [plate 52] in St Matthew's Church, Northampton. It is also surprising that there should be no sculptural forms of reclining figure and mother and child themes combined as a Reclining Mother and Child for another thirty years.

The development of the opening out of solid form can be seen in works from 1929–30 onwards. The *Half Figure* in cast concrete 1929 [plate 9], with its hollowed-out body cavity, and the slate *Head* [fig. 5] with the penetration through the eyes, give a clue of what was to follow. Moore had been impressed by the Aztec *Mask of the God Xipe Totec*. His earlier pieces in which he used the hole in a similar way as a 'formal contrast to the solid part',[6] such as *Composition* 1933 [plate 24] and *Hole and Lump* 1934 [plate 27], remain less figurative than the Aztec mask. The holes have no immediate representational reference. They are carved for inventive sculptural reasons, not just as spaces between arms and body or legs and ground or as features on a face. Not until the Reclining Figures of 1935–6 [see, for example, plate 35] did Moore begin this opening out

Fig. 5
Head, 1930 [LH 89]
Slate, H 25.4 cm

Fig. 6
Two Forms, 1934 [LH 153]
Pynkado wood, L 53.3 cm

process on more figurative works. Referring to *Hole and Lump* he stated: 'I was consciously concerned with simple relationships of form: here is the hole which is the opposite to the lump. I was putting an emphasis on this consciousness of form — of sculpture not being just an imitation of nature.'[7]

The division of the solid sculptural mass into two or more pieces began around 1934, the total entity being made up sometimes of separate individual shapes connected and related by the spaces around them, or more frequently as the idea developed of one form separated out into its individual elements. A carving in Pynkado wood [fig. 6] suggests the former. A drawing now in the Rijksmuseum Kröller-Müller at Otterlo shows a derivation from the mother and child, with the larger form protecting and shielding the smaller. This theme recurs later, through *Reclining Mother and Child* 1960–61 to *Hill Arches* 1973 [plates 96 and 150].

Four Piece Composition: Reclining Figure [plate 33] in Cumberland alabaster is an example of one form separated out into its individual elements. Here the relationship between each form and the space around it becomes vital. The sculptor has extended the viewer's response to understanding the reclining figure idea to the limit. Indeed, he has perhaps felt it necessary to restate with 'clues' exactly what the eye is perceiving as it runs down and around the figure. He has indicated in semi-figurative form what he considers to be the focal point by marking the smooth polished surface of the stone with sharply incised lines. These lines appear on the side of the body, indicating the horizontal position of the reclining figure. Moore has described each element as a 'head part, leg part, body and small round form which is the umbilicus and which makes the connection'.[8] This dismemberment of the reclining figure was not taken any further for another twenty-five years. Not until the two and three piece Reclining Figures of the 1960s and much more specifically the *Large Four Piece Reclining Figure* of 1972–3 [plate 148] did Moore return to and develop this idea.

Throughout the decade he experimented with many different varieties of native wood, including beech, box, cherry, sycamore and walnut. He was also able to acquire examples of tropical hardwoods such as ebony and lignum vitae from the Commonwealth Institute in London. For the three large wood Reclining Figures he used elm. This wood was the commonest and easiest to obtain in

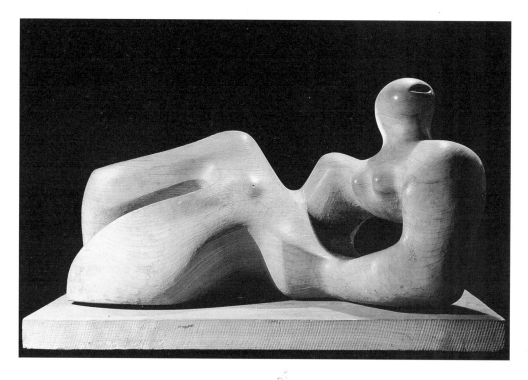

Fig. 7
Reclining Figure, 1935–6 [LH 162]
Elmwood, L 88.9 cm

large pieces. He described the making of *Reclining Figure* 1935–6 [fig. 7] as follows:

> This sculpture was carved out of a rectangular block of elmwood which was about three feet long by two feet square. The grain, of course, was along its three-foot length. Elmwood has rather a large wide grain. For this reason it is not a happy choice for small sculptures, but in a large reclining figure the horizontal grain emphasises the horizontal pose. I found there were advantages in working on a large heavy block such as this. In the early roughing-out stages, instead of using only small gouges, it was possible to work with saws and an axe. This I enjoyed and it changed my attitude to wood-carving since in the small carvings I had sometimes felt the process of production was almost like a mouse nibbling to make a hole.[9]

Immediately following this carving came *Reclining Figure* 1936 [plate 35]. With this sculpture Moore achieved his aim of opening out the mass, with the hole connecting one side to the other. Whereas the *Reclining Figure* 1929 [fig. 1] still follows the Mexican Aztec prototype of containing the figure within the solid block, the 1936 piece shows Moore's fully developed style. In 1937 Moore wrote:

> A piece of stone can have a hole through it and not be weakened
> — if the hole is of studied size, shape and direction. On the principle of the arch it can remain just as strong.
> The first hole made through a piece of stone is a revelation.
> The hole connects one side to the other, making it immediately more three-dimensional.
> A hole can itself have as much shape-meaning as a solid mass.
> Sculpture in air is possible, where the stone contains only the hole, which is the intended and considered form.
> The mystery of the hole — the mysterious fascination of caves in the hillsides and cliffs.[10]

Fig. 8
Recumbent Figure, 1938 [LH 191]
Green Hornton stone, L 1.4 m

In 1938 *Recumbent Figure* [fig. 8] was carved at Burcroft originally for the architect Serge Chermayeff, who wanted a sculpture for the intersection of his terrace and garden at Halland in Sussex. Moore said 'it was a long, low-lying building and there was an open view of the long sinuous lines of the Downs. There seemed no point in opposing all these horizontals, and I thought a tall, vertical figure would have been more of a rebuff than a contrast, and might have introduced needless drama.'[11] This is the most opened out of the stone carvings of the thirties, and perhaps of any stone carving Moore did subsequently. There is a diagonal movement through the figure from the elbow to the forward knee and then down to the base, round to the near knee and up in a figure eight through the breasts and neck to the head. Moore explained: 'I became aware of the necessity of giving outdoor sculpture a far-seeing gaze. My figure looked out across a great sweep of the Downs and her gaze gathered in the horizon.'[12]

Quickly following the *Recumbent Figure* came the 1939 *Reclining Figure* in elmwood [fig. 9]. Moore acquired the large elm trunk from a timber merchant in Canterbury. The finished sculpture was over two metres long, by far the largest piece Moore had carved and almost double the length of the 1936 *Reclining Figure* [plate 35]. It is also much more angular than either this or the *Recumbent Figure*, with not just one or two holes carved through from side to side, but a whole series moving down the length of the figure to give an impression of 'caves' and 'tunnels' isolating and at the same time linking the various elements of the body. The carving was made for the architect Berthold Lubetkin, but was later sold to Gordon Onslow Ford.

The concept of making a maquette (small model) in three dimensions as a preparatory stage to a larger work did not become apparent to Moore until about 1935. Before then his whole emphasis had been on direct carving, drawing being used as a means of expressing his ideas, literally getting them down on paper first, before he selected the ones to be realised in three dimensions. Moore later explained that by making a maquette he could study the form in his hand, have a complete grasp of its shape from all round and visualise what it would be like in full size. An exception to direct carving is the earliest major Reclining Figure in metal to have survived, *Reclining Figure* 1931, which was modelled and then cast in lead [illustrated here in bronze, plate 20].

After 1935 the idea might still appear first in a drawing but it would then be modelled in small scale. Once modelled, of necessity in some unpermanent

Fig. 9
Reclining Figure, 1939 [LH 210]
Elmwood, L 2.6 m

material like clay or plaster, the next step was to have it cast in metal to give durability. The story about Moore borrowing and ruining his wife Irina's saucepans to melt lead needed for casting comes from this period — Moore and his assistant, Bernard Meadows, set up their own foundry at Burcroft and from these home-made lead casts developed the practice of having editions in bronze produced at professional bronze foundries. Carving was still paramount for Moore at the outbreak of war, although the number of maquettes modelled and later cast had increased dramatically from 1937.

The first of Moore's stringed figures was *Stringed Relief* [fig. 10], made in part from a beechwood shoe-tree he had bought in a London street-market. As a group of work the stringed figures span just over two years and range in size from under ten to over fifty centimetres. Some are carved (for example, plate 41), others modelled and later cast in lead or bronze [plates 36 and 40], and some were wired rather than strung. Moore described their development:

> Undoubtedly the source of my stringed figures was the Science Museum. Whilst a student at the Royal College of Art I became involved in machine art which in those days had its place in modern art. Although I was interested in the work of Léger, and the Futurists, who exploited mechanical forms, I was never directly influenced by machinery as such. Its interest for me lies in its capacity for movement, which, after all, is its function. I was fascinated by the mathematical models I saw there, which had been made to illustrate the difference of the form that is half way between a square and a circle. One model had a square at one end with twenty holes along each side, making eighty holes in all. Through these holes strings were threaded and led to a circle with the same number of holes at the other end. A plane interposed through the middle shows the form that is half way between a square and a circle. One end could also be twisted to produce forms that would be terribly difficult to draw on a flat surface. It wasn't the scientific study of these models but the ability to look through the strings as with a bird cage and to see one form within another which excited me.[13]

Moore took part in the major group exhibitions throughout the decade. The *Plastik* exhibition held at the Kunsthaus, Zurich, in the summer of 1931 included three works by him. He was a founder member of Unit One and exhibited with

Fig. 10
Stringed Relief, 1937 [LH 182]
Beech wood and string, H 49.5 cm

Fig. 11
Spanish Prisoner, c. 1939 [CGM 3]
Lithograph, 365 × 305 mm

Fig. 12
September 3rd 1939, 1939 [HMF 1551]
Pencil, white wax crayon,
watercolour, coloured crayons, pen
and Indian ink, 306 × 398 mm

them at the Mayor Gallery in London in 1934 and was on the English Committee of the International Surrealist Exhibition held at the New Burlington Galleries in 1936, to which he sent three drawings and four sculptures (two carvings, one lead and one reinforced concrete). Among the artists who came to London for the exhibition were Arp, Dalí, Magritte, Miró and Tanguy. Moore had met Giacometti, Lipchitz and Zadkine by 1933 and Max Ernst visited his studio in 1936. A year later he and Irina visited Paris and went to Picasso's studio with Breton, Éluard, Ernst and Giacometti. In Amsterdam in 1938 he exhibited in the *Abstract Art* exhibition at the Stedelijk Museum. But Europe was moving steadily towards war. The influx of refugees had begun. Unit One had been a purely English movement, but the arrival in London of Naum Gabo in 1935 meant that its successor movement, Circle, was more international in outlook.

Moore signed the Surrealist manifesto in 1936, which urged the end of non-intervention in Spain, and in 1937 he became a member of the English Surrealist Group. He and Irina made their only visit to Spain in 1934, visiting Madrid, Toledo and Barcelona, and the caves at Altamira. Three years later Moore made his first lithograph, *Spanish Prisoner* [fig. 11], which was to have been sold in aid of Spanish prisoners of war held in French detention camps. But the outbreak of war put an end to the project and only a few trial proof copies remain.

The drawing inscribed 'September 3rd 1939' [fig. 12] of imaginary bathers wearing gasmasks in the sea off Dover is a horrific reminder that the thirties were nearly over and the Second World War had begun. At the outbreak of war, Moore continued to teach at Chelsea until the college was evacuated to Northampton. The Moores stayed in Hampstead but moved from Parkhill Road to No. 7, Mall Studios when Barbara Hepworth, now married to Ben Nicholson, left London for St Ives. Moore stopped carving, as Burcroft was now in a restricted area, which made movement in and out difficult. The cottage was let for the duration of the war and sold soon after. Moore intended doing war work with Graham Sutherland and applied to Chelsea Polytechnic for training in precision-toolmaking. While waiting to begin he started his war drawings. The application came to nothing and Moore was later appointed an Official War Artist. During October 1940 the Moores, who had been staying with friends at Much Hadham in Hertfordshire, returned to London to find their studio damaged by bombing. They went back to Much Hadham where their friends told them about a house nearby at Perry Green that was up for sale. Using the money paid by Gordon Onslow Ford for the *Reclining Figure* [fig. 9], they put a deposit on the house in which they were to live for the rest of their lives.

Henry Moore: 1940–1986

Julian Stallabrass

During and after the war, Moore's work became more and more widely seen and increasingly acceptable to the general public. While there were still controversies, particularly over abstraction, Moore established an unrivalled reputation as the quasi-official voice of British sculpture. It was a remarkable transformation for a sculptor on the extreme edge of the avant-garde, who was connected with both abstraction and Surrealism, and for a country which had up to this point proved comparatively hostile ground for modernism.

For many avant-garde artists, the war meant at once disruption and opportunity. While materials and working conditions were restricted, the government-run War Artists' Advisory Committee (W.A.A.C.) offered commissions, and exhibitions which reached a wide audience. Since the W.A.A.C. concerned itself only with propagandist documentation, not war memorials, Moore's sculpture was inappropriate for commission. In any case Moore, like other sculptors, found it difficult to obtain materials in the early years of the war. Instead he made drawings of the figures huddled in the London Underground tunnels used during the war as bomb shelters [figs. 13, 14]. These drawings proved very popular when exhibited by the W.A.A.C. and in this way Moore's work was first drawn to the attention of a wider public. In these exhibitions, modernist art received something of an official sanction: the drawings were shown in the grand setting of the National Gallery, from which the permanent collection had been removed for safe keeping. The Shelter drawings were collected in a book and reproduced on cards, giving them an even wider currency: their success led the W.A.A.C. to commission Moore to make a further series of drawings of coalminers.

The artist's increasing popularity was not just a matter of the wider exposure of his work. The Shelter drawings can be linked to a broader trend towards a revival of Romanticism in British art at this time. Moore's drawings exhibited the necessary Neo-Romantic qualities of readability, concentration on the human figure, the prominent use of colour and of a manifestly worked surface, a surface which bore traces of the process of creation, and which presented this process as part of the artist's sensibility. Avant-garde distortion of the figure became

Fig. 13
Shelter Drawing: Sleeping Figures,
1941 [HMF 1816]
Pencil, watercolour wash, black wax crayon, pen and Indian ink,
303 × 308 mm

Fig. 14
Moore in the London Underground,
1943 [copyright Lee Miller]

a register of the common tragic experience of the war: it was seen not as arbitrary and inhuman distortion but as a communal expression of suffering.

The years following the war saw the gradual rise of Moore's reputation to the level where he became the most pre-eminent British artist, and a figure of international renown. To some extent this success had its roots in the war years with the retrospective exhibition of his work at Temple Newsam, Leeds [fig. 15], in 1941 and his first solo exhibition in the United States at the Buchholz Gallery, New York, in 1943. The retrospective exhibition at The Museum of Modern Art in New York in 1946 was a breakthrough in establishing Moore's international reputation. Another important step in this development was the publication in 1944 of the first volume of the catalogue raisonné of his work, with an introductory essay by the prominent critic Herbert Read, an exceptional project for a sculptor of Moore's age, and one commented on by critics at the time. It was followed by a sequence of uniform volumes documenting Moore's sculptural output.

An essential component in the transformation of the radical avant-garde sculptor into a figure who seemed almost to be the official voice of British establishment culture was the perception of a more human content in his work. It was argued that the inhuman and repellent figures of the thirties had given way to a more sympathetic portrayal of the human condition. These readings were encouraged in part by the Shelter drawings but also by the large-scale sculptural projects that Moore engaged in during the forties. These included *Memorial Figure* 1945–6 [plate 54], which was made as a monument to Christopher Martin of the Dartington Hall community and consisted of a heavy, monumental figure with traditional drapery, a new departure for Moore; and *Family Group* 1948–9 [plate 53], a conventional depiction of familial values, placed in front of a curved wall in Barclay School, Stevenage, one of many new schools built in this period. Most important was the *Madonna and Child* 1943–4 [plate 52], commissioned by Canon Walter Hussey for St Matthew's Church in Northampton. Canon Hussey was later to commission Graham Sutherland to paint a Crucifixion (1946) for the same church. All these pieces are quite conventional depictions of traditional subjects with a 'humanist' reference. They were placed in settings that in themselves spoke of social solidarity. Moore wrote of how he had responded to the flexibility required for public

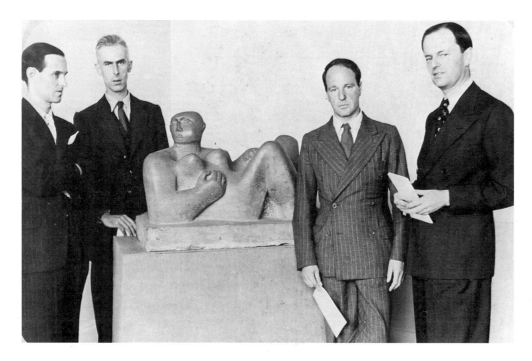

Fig. 15
Temple Newsam exhibition, Leeds, 1941. Left to right: Graham Sutherland, John Piper, Moore and Kenneth Clark

18

commissions and how he had adapted his original conception to fit the 'function' of the work.[14] The pieces accorded well with a consensus view of the unity and harmony of the nation and the caring roles adopted by the state, family and individuals within it. The themes of these public works were reflected in Moore's smaller pieces, such as the series depicting a mother and child on a rocking chair in 1950. The mother and child had been an insistent theme in Moore's work and was to continue to be so: the making of family groups at this time and of the three-figure pieces [fig. 16] that derive from them may also have been stimulated by the birth of Moore's only child, Mary, in March 1946. Herbert Read wrote that the Shelter drawings proved the 'inherent humanism' of his earlier work,[15] and this was a reading that sought retrospectively to validate Moore's earlier modernist work.

For some though, notably Nikolaus Pevsner, this move towards humanism in Moore's work was the direct consequence of a retreat from modernist forms: it was not that the war had led people to see the human element of modernism but rather that the avant-garde had abandoned modernism for a humanist view of the people. Pevsner wrote that Moore's solitary art bewildered the public, who could hardly be expected to communicate with an artist so apparently out of sympathy with the individual. Moore's work was formally beautiful, but except for the Northampton Madonna, inhuman.[16] It should be noted that not even the Shelter drawings were universally seen as registers of Moore's 'humanism': for some the portrayal of tragedy was so harsh as to be unsympathetic. These disturbing images of the shelterers were, for many people, difficult to accept as appropriate war images.[17]

Modernist critics reacted to the Pevsner view not by challenging its premise but by attempting to show that Moore had indeed returned to modernism and, in doing so, had abandoned his wartime, humanist concerns. There was some evidence that could be used to support such a view. Moore received a commission to make a major piece for the Festival of Britain, Labour's attempt to cheer up the populace during the long period of austerity that followed the war. The displays and the modernist buildings that housed them embodied an optimistic and whimsical vision of the future, of benign technology and shining and weightless architecture. There was much play on polished aluminium surfaces and suspended structures. Moore's figure was given a prominent position opposite

Fig. 16
Henry and Mary Moore in 1953 with
Family Group, 1948–9 [pl. 53]

19

the entrance to the Festival. *Reclining Figure: Festival* 1951 [see plate 64] was a disquieting, avant-garde piece which seemed to mark a break with Moore's 'humanism' and was indeed reminiscent of the lead figures of the thirties. Its features, especially the eyes that, Janus-like, stare out from either side of the split head, are inhuman. The sculpture is made up of discrete units, articulated like the body of an insect. The forms are reminiscent of bone but are marked with carved striations. The figure has the aspect of something undecided between life and representation, as if it were the product of a Pygmalion working in reverse. It also has a funerary element, for the motif of the reclining figure on a base relates to the sculpted cover of a sarcophagus. In all it can be read as a memorial sculpture, as a tragic and cathartic piece. In the context of the Festival, Moore's figure could have seemed harsh and forbidding: it was a work that looked back to the war as well as forward to a future that was not universally seen as a bright technocratic dream.

There was a current of unease and repugnance running through views of Moore's postwar sculpture, counter to humanist readings of his work. This resistance has often been presented as simply a conservative reluctance to accept formal innovation. Many of those who admired Moore's skill and formal inventiveness, nevertheless still found the works in some way repellent. They saw this as quite separate from any issue of form. Even Moore's greatest advocates felt the need to account for the disturbing nature of his work. There was a widespread assumption that these works in some way reduced humanity to a lower form of life, immobilised it and even brought it to a deathlike state.[18] This view was far from uncommon and it was used particularly to explain the effect of works such as the Helmet Heads [plates 58, 59], *Falling Warrior* 1956–7 [plate 85] and other pieces related to them, pieces of a masculine and aggressive character, which seemed at once paranoid and protecting. Multiple readings of the Helmet Heads are certainly possible: they can be seen as the soul in the body, the foetus in the womb, the child hugged to the mother, the endangered being which seeks protection and yet seeks to endanger, and as death itself. In an interview Moore restated the connection of the Heads with armour and said that in addition they were connected to the mother and child and to the embryo in the womb, an idea which had what he called 'fundamental human depth'.[19] Moore himself certainly contributed to a universalist reading of his works.

There was however a strong trend in contemporary criticism towards defusing the frightening nature of Moore's work, and this applied as much to those who attacked it as to those who praised it. The most common avenue of attack, even from his admirers, was the charge of its being too suave, too good to be true. The pristine quality of the surfaces was associated with the supposedly uncomplicated nature of the work. Patrick Heron commented on the extreme smoothness of Moore's surfaces which led to vacuity.[20] Basil Taylor, Heron's opponent in a debate on Moore staged in the magazine *Encounter*, also highlighted this aspect, describing Moore's suave surfaces as being as inexpressive as a finely turned chair leg.[21] Douglas Cooper and Clement Greenberg had similar complaints, Cooper saying that Moore's real trouble was that he was frightened of being vulgar, Greenberg that his sculpture was so tasteful that there was no difficulty or surprise about his art, that it was the work of a 'sincere academic modern'.[22] For the left-wing critic John Berger, readings of Moore's work as tragic or apocalyptic were too general: he explained Moore's (and Sutherland's) great popularity by what he described as the 'sentimental, highbrow fashion for projecting crises of conscience and introspection on to the timeless processes of nature', in a way that was comforting because the material details of these crises were lost.[23] There is a sense in which the very exigencies of the postwar period are used to give Moore's work a more universal than specific reference, and thus defuse them as political or social statements. For Moore to become established as a sculptor acceptable to a wide audience, it was necessary that the disquieting aspects of his work be rendered powerless. This was achieved partly through sheer familiarity, partly through the strategies of the critics. The claim that disturbing deformations are merely formal devices shifts the focus of any reading from the experience of the viewer to the formal sensibility of the artist. Protestations about Moore's academicism ironically reinforced his position as an elder statesman in relation to a younger and wilder avant-garde.

Those looking for a darker, inhuman side to Moore's work had clear examples to support their view. Among them were the totem-like presences of the Upright Motives of 1955–6, which are comparable to some of Sutherland's standing figures. They appeared to combine mechanistic and stumpy, fleshy forms and, like totem poles, to be composed of heterogeneous parts assembled in a way that made no anatomical sense. From 1949 Sutherland had worked on standing figures, such as *Standing Forms against a Hedge* [fig. 17] which is a sculptural object placed on a plinth, modelled in consistent light, and with metallic elements. As in Moore's *Three Standing Figures* 1953 [plate 66], Sutherland sometimes grouped these presences in threes. Both feature Surrealistic, alien, metallic and bony personages. The link between Sutherland and Moore is less important as a formal influence than as an expression of a similar sensibility in relation to the events of the war and, more generally, to the attitude the work of art assumes in relation to the viewer. Moore referred to a knife-edge tension in some of his titles, to an acute formal and emotional balance: Sutherland made similar statements about the ambiguity of his works which he claimed could be seen as positive or negative: 'People have said that my most typical images express a dark and pessimistic outlook.... the precarious tension of opposites — happiness and unhappiness, beauty and ugliness, so near the point of balance — are capable of being interpreted according to the predilections and needs of the beholder — with enthusiasm and delight, or abhorrence, as with the taste of bitter-sweet fruit.'[24] This may help us to begin to understand the duality of Moore's work and of the criticism about it which, as we have seen, ranges at the extremes from utter repugnance to utter indifference. In 1937 Moore had written of the fundamental importance of vitality to sculpture — of sculpture taking on a human or animal character which forms the basis of criteria for judging its formal

Fig. 17
Graham Sutherland's *Standing Forms Against a Hedge*, 1950. Collection: The Arts Council of Great Britain

success.[25] This can account for both the humanism and the disturbing element of deformation in Moore's work. The two are aspects of the same thing. It is possible to construct other oppositions within Moore's work, certainly between masculine and feminine, protection and aggression. It may be that the sculpture occupies the point of balance between such oppositions or, if a dominance of one element can be discovered, it may be that the relationship is more complex.

It could be argued that Moore made conscious attempts to resolve such dichotomies in monumental sculptures such as the *Unesco Reclining Figure* 1957–8 [plate 86], his largest carving to date, made for the Paris headquarters of the organisation on a scale to compete with this huge building. The carving in Roman travertine marble is modernist and subject to deformation, yet its static, calm nature and its monumentality mitigate any disturbance for the viewer. Carving the Unesco figure also first brought Moore to the Henraux marble works near Forte dei Marmi in Italy. He continued to visit the works, eventually building a house nearby, and regularly supervising the carving of large pieces in marble. The Unesco piece marked the beginning of the founding of an atelier by Moore, of the regular use of assistants responsible for much of the work on the enlargement of ideas originally worked out in the form of hand-held maquettes. These large pieces were done in partnership with the sculpture assistants at Perry Green, the carvers at Henraux, and the craftsmen at the Noack foundry in Berlin [fig. 18] and the Singer foundry in Basingstoke.

Large abstract works, despite their organic references, could not be read in the same way as the deformed figures. The sixties saw Moore developing a number of original abstract ideas, a notable change from the figure pieces of the fifties. Sculptures such as *Locking Piece* 1963–4 [plates 101–103], *Knife Edge Two Piece* 1962–5 [plates 108, 109], *The Arch* 1963–9 [plate 107] and *Sheep Piece* 1971–2 [plate 145] have an organic reference (often signalled in the titles) but are certainly not as such related to the human form. Again dichotomies are established between hard and soft, mechanistic and fleshy, the aggressive and the yielding. *Oval with Points* 1968–70 [plate 134] is like an armoured creature turned inside out, exposing a soft, rounded exterior to the world while being aggressively angled on its interior. These abstract pieces are exemplary of Moore's later eccentric and marginal position in relation to modernism. Their size, the heaviness of their movements and the durability of their material, in addition to their placement outside government buildings and the headquarters of major commercial enterprises, gave them the air of official monuments. It was this resolved, self-assured aspect of Moore's later work that led younger sculptors and critics to express misgivings about his work. One of

Fig. 18
Moore at the Noack Foundry, Berlin, with *Upright Internal/External Form*, 1952–3 [pl. 73]

Fig. 19
Florence, 1972: Forte di Belvedere, Mostra di Henry Moore. Assembly of Square Form with Cut, 1969 [see pl. 136]

the most notable of these was Anthony Caro, a former assistant to Moore and a pioneer of steel sculpture, who wrote what was ostensibly a celebration of Moore's work for the *Observer* newspaper in 1960 on the occasion of a retrospective exhibition at the Whitechapel Gallery in London. Caro wrote that Moore's reputation as a great public figure masked any view of his achievements as a real artist, that for younger sculptors their relation to Moore was in part clouded by 'family reasons' and that they resisted coming to terms with this 'father figure'. Caro implied that there was on the part of the younger generation an Oedipal resistance to the artist who was after all the father of modern sculpture in Britain. When controversy later arose over a gift of his work made by Moore to the Tate Gallery (and the need for an extension apparently to house it) the attacks were on the same lines. Many younger artists wrote a collective letter to *The Times* claiming that Moore was out of step with modern society in representing the artist in a 'heroic and monumental role', associated with the triumph of modern art in society.[26] While his younger contemporaries were welding constructed sculptures, making land and performance art, questioning the boundaries of the gallery and the very notion of the work of art, and in the case of John Latham destroying books, Moore continued to erect large monumental sculptures in highly durable materials.

It was not merely the permanence, monumentality and placement of Moore's sculptures which made him appear an authoritarian figure to the younger generation, but also the numerous honours heaped on him by state and academic institutions at home and abroad, capped, perhaps, by his elevation to the Order of Merit in 1963. Exhibitions of Moore's work also took on a monumental scale, especially the massive, spectacularly sited show in Florence in 1972, where large works placed in the Forte di Belvedere could be viewed against the background of the city [fig. 19].

The ambiguity established by the dichotomies in Moore was not however the stuff of monuments. Oppositions between organic and abstract are often established and these are connected with another opposition between the real and the represented. The organic reference of the works was often derived from Moore's continued use of found objects, notably bones, from which *Standing Figure: Knife Edge* 1961 [see working model, plate 97] and *Three Piece Sculpture: Vertebrae* 1968–9 [plate 128] were derived. He made a small series of figures the torsos of which were made up of leaves in 1952, and later, in 1975, the shell skirt series. This use of found objects, both natural and manufactured, to some extent ruptures the unity of representation in the works.

Such dichotomies take on formal guises. A common theme in Moore criticism, and one to which the Helmet Heads are relevant, is the stress on the idea of the sculpture growing, being a product of forces pressing on it from within. There is a feeling of something stirring under the skin of the sculpture. It was a theme linked through biomorphism to Surrealism and was a key concern of Arp, whom Moore met and admired.[27] Moore himself encouraged such an appreciation of his sculpture, writing about the forces and power that strained from the inside of a piece: 'Hardness, projection outwards, gives tension, force, and vitality.'[28] He also thought that the sculpture should make the viewer feel that what he was seeing 'contains within itself its own organic energy thrusting outwards... It should always give the impression, whether carved or modelled, of having grown organically, created by pressure from within.'[29] For Patrick Heron, the Reclining Figures contained complex formal movements beneath the skin of the sculpture.[30] He put it thus: 'in one's eye the image swells and changes, contracts and changes, as one steps around the sculpture standing there, before one, in space.'[31] In making a sculpture ever more complex, Moore stretches and distorts but never ruptures the membrane that surrounds it. The Lincoln Center figure [LH 519] [see working model, plates 104, 105] appears to contain a frank opposition between standing and recumbent elements with the thrusting motion of its upright piece. This is however only apparent from certain viewpoints, for the sculpture changes radically when seen from different angles. The masculine is written into an aspect of this ostensibly female figure and, like repressed material in the unconscious, is only visible at certain times. Such an opposition is made quite explicit in *Sheep Piece* [plate 145], where the first word of the title must be read in the plural.

A development of forces playing within the unitary skin of the sculpture was to divide the piece into separate units. As we have seen, Moore's division of the figure into independent parts had a precedent in *Four Piece Composition: Reclining Figure* [plate 33] of 1934 but in the sixties it was developed as an insistent theme. The reclining figures which are divided into parts have usually been read in formal terms as a development of the opening up of space in the body of the sculpture, first with holes and then in a more radical way where the figure delineates a space, as in *Reclining Figure: Festival* [plate 64]. The Lincoln Center figure and other pieces such as the maquette *Two Piece Reclining Figure* [fig. 20] appear as though a single figure has been eroded into separate pieces over time. Others are made up of parts that appear in a more forthright opposition. Given the attraction that Moore's work has had for those wishing to make psychoanalytical readings, it is easy to see such works in terms of competing elements within the figure — pieces that perhaps have a separate sexual identity, or in the case of eroded figures, as undergoing a process of change or even loss of identity. Some pieces appear to have been worked on by external forces, and to a degree to have succumbed to them. Others embody Moore's dictum about the sculpture seeming to work from the inside out, to embody a force that strains from within against the skin of the work: given the play of movement and resistance in these pieces it is plainly possible to read them in terms of forces and balances in the Freudian psyche. Even the mother and child theme was sometimes treated in an ambiguous way by Moore. In *Mother and Child* 1953 [plate 69] a baby with an angular head and wide-open mouth is held at bay, Laocoon-like, by an equally inhuman mother grasping its snakelike body. Devouring and aggressive relations between mother and child are presented here and in some of a series of graphics he made on the theme in 1983. The way that the roles of the family members change from protection to aggression, which

Fig. 20
Two Piece Reclining Figure: Maquette No. 1, 1960 [LH 473]

is linked to the wider issue of shifting sexual identities, has to be seen in the light of the widespread adherence to psychoanalytic theory among the British avant-garde. Herbert Read, a close friend of the sculptor's, was a committed Jungian. In 1959 Erich Neumann wrote the widely read *The Archetypal Work of Henry Moore*, a Jungian interpretation of the subject.

The mechanisation of the figure is highly apparent in *Large Four Piece Reclining Figure* [plate 148], with its rimmed units making up two highly polished bipartite elements which gesture energetically at each other. The separation of these units into parts, their interrelation, and the changing aspects of the sculpture when seen in the round, set up complex combinations of oppositions. In *Two Piece Reclining Figure: Points* [fig. 21] two elements strain towards each other, culminating in bullet-shaped points. Moore's concern with formal incident sets the pieces of the sculpture in dramatic opposition and leads him to articulate the elements in a radical fashion. Given that the pieces can never touch, and the articulation of discrete elements which suggests the mechanical, there is here a curious repetition of the Dada bachelor machine, of an impotent mechanism beneath the formal play.

It may be that Moore's work can be seen as uncanny, that beneath its familiarity and what some critics have identified as its slickness is secreted a set of repressed themes. These themes concern traditionally masculine attributes of aggression and action, but also unresolved actions (including the creative act) and the inhuman mechanisation of the self. The formalist, balanced and feminine character of Moore's work contains aspects of its opposite. Recognising this is not so much a matter of simply uncovering a different set of concerns in the sculpture and forgetting its manifest character, but of grasping the fundamental instability in its themes. In striving to give his sculpture formal dynamism in the round, Moore rendered the very identity of his work fluid. This constant shifting of themes, including those that concern creativity itself, calls into question the nature of the work of art as a resolved piece. Moore's very success, however, and the use of so much of his sculpture as monuments, has compromised the shifting aspect of his work, throwing weight decisively on the side of familiarity.

Fig. 21
Two Piece Reclining Figure: Points,
1969–70 [LH 606]

25

NOTES

LH numbers refer to *Henry Moore: Complete Sculpture* (6 vols), London 1944–88; HMF numbers to the drawing archive at the Henry Moore Foundation; CGM numbers to Cramer, Grant, Mitchinson (eds), *Henry Moore: Catalogue of Graphic Work* (4 vols), Geneva 1973–88.

Sculptures in the catalogue referred to in the text are identified by their plate numbers; other works illustrated are referred to by their figure numbers.

1. The first is probably *Head of a Girl* 1923 [LH 15], the second is uncatalogued and the third as yet unidentified.

2. *Auden Poems/Moore Lithographs*, London 1974.

3. Herbert Read (ed.), *Unit 1: The Modern Movement in English Architecture, Painting and Sculpture*, London 1934, pp. 29–30.

4. For further explanation see Alan G. Wilkinson, *The Moore Collection in the Art Gallery of Ontario*, Toronto 1979, p. 45.

5. The problem of support for sculpture always interested Moore: see J. D. Morse, 'Henry Moore Comes to America', *The Magazine of Art*, 1947, vol. 40, no. 3.

6. *Henry Moore at the British Museum*, London 1981, p. 74.

7. *Henry Moore: Wood Sculptures*, photographs by Gemma Levine, London, New York 1983.

8. For further explanation see R. Morpeth, *Illustrated Catalogue of Acquisitions, The Tate Gallery 1976–8*, London 1979, pp. 116–18.

9. *Henry Moore: Wood Sculptures*.

10. Henry Moore, 'The Sculptor Speaks', *Listener*, 1937, vol. XVIII, no. 449.

11. 'Sculpture in the Open Air', a talk by Henry Moore for the British Council reproduced in Philip James (ed.), *Henry Moore on Sculpture*, London 1966.

12. Ibid.

13. John Hedgecoe (ed.), *Henry Moore*, London 1968.

14. Address given in Venice, 1952; reproduced in James, *Henry Moore on Sculpture*, pp. 86–7.

15. Introduction by Herbert Read in David Sylvester (ed.), *Henry Moore: Sculpture and Drawings 1921–1948*, London 1944, p. xxvii.

16. Nikolaus Pevsner, 'Thoughts on Henry Moore', *The Burlington Magazine*, vol. LXXXVI, no. 503, February 1945, p. 48.

17. Dennis Rudder claimed that Moore's work was so extreme that many people found it difficult to deal with. Quoted in Eric Newton, *War through Artists' Eyes. Paintings and Drawings by British War Artists*, London 1945, p. 9.

18. See for instance Robin Ironside, 'Painting since 1939', in Arnold L. Haskell, Dilys Powell, Rollo Myers and Robin Ironside, *Since 1939. Ballet. Films. Music. Painting*, London 1948, pp. 173–4.

19. Paul Waldo Schwarz, *The Hand and Eye of the Sculptor*, New York, Washington, London 1969, p. 201.

20. Patrick Heron and Basil Taylor, 'Henry Moore — Pro and Con', *The Arts*, no. 1, 1946, pp. 53–4.

21. Ibid., pp. 55, 57.

22. Douglas Cooper, 'Selected Notices', *Horizon*, vol. X, no. 60, December 1944, p. 428; Clement Greenberg, 'Art', *The Nation*, 8 February 1947.

23. John Berger, 'Piltdown Sculpture', *New Statesman and Nation*, 27 February 1954.

24. Graham Sutherland, *Listener*, xlvi, 1951, p. 378.

25. Moore, 'The Sculptor Speaks'; James, *Henry Moore on Sculpture*, p. 68.

26. *The Times*, 26 May 1967. The letter was signed by 41 artists including Gillian Ayres, Anthony Caro, Patrick Caulfield, Elisabeth Frink, Howard Hodgkin, Phillip King, John Latham, Edouardo Paolozzi and William Tucker.

27. Moore met Arp at The Museum of Modern Art, New York, in 1946.

28. Henry Moore, 'Some Notes on Space and Form in Sculpture', in Felix H. Man, *Eight European Artists*, London, Melbourne, Toronto 1954, n.p.

29. Moore interviewed by Edward Roditi, *Observer*, 10 April 1960; James, *Henry Moore on Sculpture*, p. 58.

30. Patrick Heron, *The Changing Forms of Art*, London 1955, p. 208.

31. Heron and Taylor, 'Henry Moore — Pro and Con', p. 53.

CHRONOLOGY

This chronology lists only the major events in Henry Moore's life; a more detailed version is available from the Henry Moore Foundation.

1898 *30 July*: Henry Spencer Moore born at Castleford, Yorkshire.

1902–10 Attended elementary school in Castleford.

1910 Won scholarship to Castleford Secondary (later Grammar) School.

1915 Received Cambridge Leaving Certificate; trained as an elementary school teacher by practice in local schools.

1917 Enlisted in the Civil Service Rifles, 15th London Regiment; gassed at the Battle of Cambrai.

1918 Attended army physical training course; promoted to instructor and lance corporal; volunteered for active service but reached France just before Armistice Day.

1920 Sculpture department set up at Leeds with Moore the sole student.

1921 Won scholarship to the Royal College of Art, London, to study sculpture.

1923 Visited Paris where he studied Cézanne in the Auguste Pellerin collection.

1924 Took part in mixed exhibition at the Redfern Gallery, London; awarded Royal College of Art travelling scholarship; accepted seven-year appointment as instructor at the RCA Sculpture School.

1925 Visited Paris, Rome, Florence, Pisa, Siena, Assisi, Padua, Ravenna and Venice.

1926 Exhibited in a group show at St George's Gallery, London.

1927 Participated in a group exhibition at the Beaux-Arts Gallery, London.

1928 First one-man exhibition at the Warren Gallery, London.

1929 Married Irina Radetsky; completed relief sculpture on the north wall of the Headquarters of the London Underground.

1930 Elected to the '7 and 5 Society'; exhibited with the Young Painters' Society and the London Group and in the British Pavilion at the Venice Biennale.

1931 Resigned from teaching post at the Royal College of Art; first sale abroad, to the Museum für Kunst und Gewerbe, Hamburg; second one-man exhibition at the Leicester Galleries, London.

1932 Became first head of sculpture in new department at Chelsea School of Art.

1933 Chosen to be a member of Unit One; exhibition at the Leicester Galleries, London.

1934 Contributed to 'Unit One' exhibition at the Mayor Gallery, London; visited Altamira, Madrid, Barcelona, Les Eyzies; publication of the first monograph on his work (by Herbert Read).

1935 Exhibition at Zwemmer's, London.

1936 Served on the Organising Committee and participated in the International Surrealist Exhibition at the New Burlington Galleries, London.

1938 Took part in the International Exhibition of Abstract Art at the Stedelijk Museum, Amsterdam.

1940 Began shelter drawings in London Underground; moved from London to Perry Green, Hertfordshire; exhibition at the Leicester Galleries, London.

1941 Appointed an Official War Artist; appointed a Trustee of the Tate Gallery (1941–56); first retrospective exhibition at Temple Newsam House, Leeds, with Graham Sutherland and John Piper.

1942 Appointed to the Art Panel of the Council for the Encouragement of Music and Art (later the Arts Council of Great Britain).

1943 First one-man exhibition abroad, at Buchholz Gallery, New York.

1944 Installation of *Madonna and Child* in St Matthew's Church, Northampton.

1945 Created Honorary Doctor of Literature, University of Leeds.

1946 Birth of his only child, Mary; installation of *Memorial Figure* at Dartington Hall, Devon; first visit to New York for travelling retrospective which opened at The Museum of Modern Art.

1947 Travelling exhibition opened at the Art Gallery of New South Wales, Sydney.

1948 Appointed member of the Royal Fine Art Commission (1948–71); visited Venice for one-man exhibition in the British Pavilion at the XXIV Biennale, where he won the International Prize for Sculpture.

1949 Exhibition at Palais des Beaux-Arts, Brussels, which travelled 1949–1951 to Paris, Amsterdam, Hamburg, Düsseldorf, Bern and Athens.

1951 First retrospective at the Tate Gallery; *Reclining Figure: Festival* exhibited at the Festival of Britain; toured Greece on the occasion of his exhibition in Athens.

1953 Installation of *Draped Reclining Figure* and *Time/Life Screen* in Bond Street, London; awarded International Sculpture Prize at the 2nd São Paulo Biennale; visited Brazil and Mexico; exhibition at the Institute of Contemporary Arts, London.

1954 Commissioned to design a relief in brick for the new Bouwcentrum, Rotterdam.

1955 Appointed Member of the Order of the Companions of Honour; appointed Trustee of the National Gallery, London (1955–74).

1956 Visited The Netherlands on the occasion of the 350th anniversary of the birth of Rembrandt.

1957 Awarded prize at the Carnegie International, Pittsburgh; awarded the Stefan Lochner Medal by the City of Cologne.

1958 Installation of *Reclining Figure* outside the Unesco Headquarters in Paris; appointed Chairman of the Auschwitz Memorial Committee.

1959 Awarded Foreign Minister's prize, 5th Biennale, Tokyo; travelling exhibition opened at the Zachenta Gallery, Warsaw.

1960 Exhibition at the Whitechapel Gallery, London.

1961 Exhibition at the Scottish National Gallery of Modern Art, Edinburgh.

1962 Travelling exhibition opened at the Arts Council Gallery, Cambridge.

1963 Invested with the insignia of a Member of the Order of Merit (Civil Division); awarded the Antonio Feltrinelli Prize for sculpture by the Accademia Nazionale dei Lincei, Rome.

1964 Appointed member of the Arts Council of Great Britain; awarded Fine Arts Medal by the Institute of Architects in America.

1965 Visited New York for installation of *Reclining Figure* at the Lincoln Center.

1966 Visited Canada for presentation ceremony of *Three Way Piece No. 2: The Archer* in Nathan Phillips Square, Toronto; elected Fellow of the British Academy.

1967 Visited America for unveiling of *Nuclear Energy* on the University of Chicago campus; created Honorary Doctor, Royal College of Art, London.

1968 Awarded the Order of Merit by the Federal Republic of Germany; Einstein Prize by the Yeshiva University, New York; retrospective at the Tate Gallery, London, to mark his seventieth birthday; exhibition at the Rijksmuseum Kröller-Müller, Otterlo, where he received the Erasmus Prize.

1971 Visited Toronto to plan Henry Moore Sculpture Centre at Art Gallery of Ontario; elected Honorary Fellow of the Royal Institute of British Architects.

1972 Visited Italy for the opening by HRH The Princess Margaret of retrospective exhibition at Forte di Belvedere, Florence; created Cavaliere di Gran Croce dell'Ordine al Merito della Repubblica Italiana; Foreign Member of the Orden pour le Mérite für Wissenschaften und Künste, West Germany; awarded Premio Internazionale 'Le Muse', Florence.

1973 Awarded Premio Umberto Biancamano, Milan; created Commandeur de l'Ordre des Arts et des Lettres, Paris; exhibition at Los Angeles County Museum of Art.

1974 Visited Canada for the installation and opening of the Henry Moore Sculpture Centre at the Art Gallery of Ontario, Toronto.

1975 Exhibition at the Tate Gallery on occasion of gift of graphics by the artist; awarded the Kaiserring der Stadt Goslar.

1976 Exhibition of war drawings at the Imperial War Museum, London; exhibition in Zurich organised by the Zürcher Forum.

1977 Inauguration of the Henry Moore Foundation at Much Hadham; exhibition at the Orangerie des Tuileries, Paris; exhibition at the Art Gallery of Ontario, Toronto, which travelled to four locations in Japan and then to the Tate Gallery, London, in 1978.

1978 Awarded Grosse Goldene Ehrenzeichen by the City of Vienna; Austrian Medal for Science and Art; gift of thirty-six sculptures to the Tate Gallery; eightieth birthday exhibitions at the Tate Gallery, the Serpentine Gallery, London, and Bradford; *Mirror: Knife Edge* installed at the National Gallery of Art, Washington DC.

1980 Awarded the Grand Cross of the Order of Merit of the Federal Republic of Germany; *The Arch* given to the Department of the Environment for permanent position in Kensington Gardens, London.

1981 Elected full Member of Académie Européenne des Sciences, des Arts et des Lettres, Paris; travelling exhibition opened in Palacio de Velázquez, Palacio de Cristal and Parque de El Retiro, Madrid.

1982 The Henry Moore Sculpture Gallery and Centre for the Study of Sculpture opened by HM The Queen as an extension to Leeds City Art Gallery; travelling exhibition opened in Museo de Arte Moderno, Mexico City; exhibition at the Hoam Art Museum, Seoul.

1983 Awarded Mexican Order of Aguila Azteca; exhibition at The Metropolitan Museum of Art, New York.

1984 Created Commandeur de l'Ordre National de la Légion d'Honneur when President Mitterrand visited Much Hadham; travelling exhibition opened at the National Gallery, East Berlin.

1985 Awarded Bulgarian Order of St Cyril and St Methodius (First Degree).

1986 *31 August*: died at Perry Green, Hertfordshire; *18 November*: Service of Thanksgiving for the Life and Work of Henry Moore in Westminster Abbey, London.

SELECTED BIBLIOGRAPHY

CATALOGUES RAISONNÉS

Henry Moore: Complete Sculpture. Volume 1, 1921–48 (*Sculpture and Drawings*), edited by Herbert Read, 1944; revised edition 1957, edited by David Sylvester. Volume 2, 1949–54, edited by David Sylvester, 1955. Volume 3, 1955–64, edited by Alan Bowness, 1965. Volume 4, 1964–73, edited by Alan Bowness, 1977. Volume 5, 1974–80, edited by Alan Bowness, 1983. Volume 6, 1981–86, edited by Alan Bowness, 1988. Lund Humphries/Zwemmer, London.

Henry Moore: Catalogue of Graphic Work. (Volume I), 1931–72, edited by Gérald Cramer, Alistair Grant and David Mitchinson, 1973. Volume II, 1973–75, edited by Gérald Cramer, Alistair Grant and David Mitchinson, 1976. Volume III, 1976–79, edited by Patrick Cramer, Alistair Grant and David Mitchinson, 1980. Volume IV, 1980–84, edited by Patrick Cramer, Alistair Grant and David Mitchinson, 1988. Cramer, Geneva.

SELECTED PUBLICATIONS

Argan, Giulio Carlo: *Henry Moore*. First published by Fabbri, Milan 1971; Abrams, New York 1973; Praeger, New York 1974.

As the Eye Moves... A Sculpture by Henry Moore, photographs by David Finn, words by Donald Hall. Abrams, New York 1970.

Berthoud, Roger: *The Life of Henry Moore*. Faber, London; E.P. Dutton, New York 1987.

Clark, Kenneth: *Henry Moore Drawings*. Thames and Hudson, London; Harper and Row, New York 1974.

The Drawings of Henry Moore, edited by Alan G. Wilkinson. Garland, New York 1984.

Fezzi, Elda: *Henry Moore*. Hamlyn, London 1971; Crown Publishers, New York 1972.

Finn, David: *Henry Moore: Sculpture and Environment*. Abrams, New York 1976; Thames and Hudson, London 1977.

Garrould, Ann, and Valerie Power: *Henry Moore: Tapestries*. Diptych, London 1988.

Grigson, Geoffrey: *Henry Moore*. Penguin Books, Harmondsworth 1943.

Grohmann, Will: *The Art of Henry Moore*. First published by Rembrandt Verlag, Berlin 1960; Thames and Hudson, London; Abrams, New York 1960.

Hall, Donald: *Henry Moore: The Life and Work of a Great Sculptor*. Gollancz, London; Harper and Row, New York 1960.

Henry Moore, edited with photographs by John Hedgecoe, words by Henry Moore. Nelson, London; Simon and Schuster, New York 1968.

Henry Moore at the British Museum, introduction and commentary by Henry Moore, photographs by David Finn. British Museum Publications, London 1981; Abrams, New York 1982.

Henry Moore: Drawings, edited by Ann Garrould. Thames and Hudson, London; Rizzoli, New York 1988.

Henry Moore: Energy in Space, photographs by John Hedgecoe. Bruckmann, Munich; New York Graphic Society, Boston 1974.

Henry Moore: Heads, Figures and Ideas, comment by Geoffrey Grigson. Rainbird, London; New York Graphic Society, Boston 1958.

Henry Moore Maquettes, text by Erich Steingräber. Pantheon Edition, Studio Bruckmann, Munich 1978.

Henry Moore: Mother and Child Etchings, introduction by Gail Gelburd. Raymond Spencer Company, Much Hadham 1988.

Henry Moore: My Ideas, Inspiration and Life as an Artist, photographs by John Hedgecoe. Ebury Press, London; Chronicle Books, San Francisco 1986.

Henry Moore on Sculpture, edited by Philip James. Macdonald, London 1966; Viking, New York 1967, revised 1971.

Henry Moore: Sculpture, edited by David Mitchinson, introduction by Franco Russoli. Polígrafa, Barcelona; Macmillan, London; Rizzoli, New York 1981.

Henry Moore: Unpublished Drawings, edited by David Mitchinson. Fratelli Pozzo, Turin; Abrams, New York 1971.

Henry Moore: Wood Sculptures, photographs by Gemma Levine. Sidgwick and Jackson, London; Universe Books, New York 1983.

Henry Moore's Sheep Sketchbook. Thames and Hudson, London and New York 1980.

Hodin, J.P.: *Henry Moore*. First published by De Lange, Amsterdam 1956; Zwemmer, London 1958.

Homage to Henry Moore, special issue of the *XXᵉ siècle* review, edited by G. di San Lazzaro. XXᵉ Siècle, Paris; Zwemmer, London; Tudor, New York 1972.

Jianou, Ionel: *Henry Moore*. Arted, Paris; Tudor, New York 1968.

Large Two Forms: A Sculpture by Henry Moore, preface by Kenneth Clark, introduction by William T. Ylisaker, photographs by David Finn. Abbeville Press, New York 1981.

Melville, Robert: *Henry Moore: Sculpture and Drawings 1921–1969*. Thames and Hudson, London; Abrams, New York 1970.

The Moore Collection in the Art Gallery of Ontario, text by Alan G. Wilkinson. Art Gallery of Ontario, Toronto 1979; revised edition entitled *Henry Moore Remembered*, Art Gallery of Ontario/Key Porter, Toronto 1987.

Museum Without Walls: Henry Moore in New York City from the Ablah Collection, introduction by J. Carter Brown, photographs by David Finn and Amy Binder. Book of the Month Club, New York 1985.

Neumann, Erich: *The Archetypal World of Henry Moore*. Routledge, London; Pantheon Books, New York 1959; Harper and Row, New York 1965; Princeton University Press, Princeton, New Jersey 1985.

Packer, William: *Henry Moore: An Illustrated Biography*, with photographs by Gemma Levine. Weidenfeld and Nicolson, London; Grove Press, New York 1985.

Read, Herbert: *Henry Moore, Sculptor: An Appreciation*. Zwemmer, London 1934.

Read, Herbert: *Henry Moore: A Study of His Life and Work*. Thames and Hudson, London 1965; Praeger, New York 1966.

Read, Herbert: *Henry Moore: Mother and Child*. Unesco/Collins, London; New American Library, New York 1966.

Read, John: *Henry Moore: Portrait of an Artist*. Whizzard Press/André Deutsch, London; Hacker, New York 1979.

Russell, John: *Henry Moore*. Allen Lane, London; Putnam, New York 1968; revised edition, Penguin Books, Harmondsworth 1973.

Spender, Stephen: *Henry Moore: Sculptures and Landscape*, introduction by Henry Moore, photographs by Geoffrey Shakerley. First published in Norway by J.M. Stenersens, Oslo 1978; Studio Vista, London; Clarkson Potter, New York 1978.

Strachan, Walter: *Henry Moore: Animals*. Aurum Press/Bernard Jacobson, London 1983.

With Henry Moore: The Artist at Work, photographs by Gemma Levine. Sidgwick and Jackson, London; Times Books, New York 1978.

MAJOR EXHIBITION CATALOGUES

Henry Moore, text by James Johnson Sweeney. The Museum of Modern Art/Simon and Schuster, New York 1947.

Sculpture and Drawings by Henry Moore, text by David Sylvester. Arts Council of Great Britain, London 1951.

Henry Moore: Sculpture 1950–1960, text by Bryan Robertson. White-chapel Art Gallery, London 1960.

Henry Moore: Stone and Wood Carvings. Marlborough Fine Art, London 1961.

Henry Moore, text by David Sylvester. Arts Council of Great Britain, London; Praeger, New York 1968.

Henry Moore. Rijksmuseum Kröller-Müller, Otterlo/Museum Boymans-Van Beuningen, Rotterdam 1968.

Henry Moore Exhibition in Japan, 1969, text by David Thompson. Mainichi Newspapers, Tokyo 1969.

Henry Moore: Drawings, Watercolours, Gouaches, text by Alan G. Wilkinson. Galerie Beyeler, Basel 1970.

Henry Moore: Carvings 1961–1970, Bronzes 1961–1970. M. Knoedler, New York/Marlborough Gallery, New York 1970.

Elephant Skull: Original Etchings by Henry Moore. Galerie Cramer, Geneva 1970.

Moore e Firenze, edited by Giovanni Carandente. Il Bisonte, Florence 1972, revised 1979.

Henry Moore in America, text by Henry J. Seldis. Los Angeles County Museum of Art, Los Angeles/Praeger, New York; Phaidon, London 1973.

Auden Poems/Moore Lithographs. British Museum, London 1974.

Henry Moore by Henry Moore Exhibition, text by John Russell. Mainichi Newspapers, Tokyo 1974.

Henry Moore: Skulptur, Teckning, Grafik 1923–1975, text by Anne Seymour. Henie-Onstad Kunstsenter, Høvikodden/Kulturhuset, Stockholm/Nordjyllands Kunstmuseum, Ålborg 1975.

Henry Moore: Graphics in the Making, text by Pat Gilmour. Tate Gallery/Idea Books, London 1975.

Expo Henry Moore, edited by Georg Müller. Zürcher Forum, Zurich 1976.

The Drawings of Henry Moore, text by Alan G. Wilkinson. Art Gallery of Ontario, Toronto 1977; Tate Gallery, London 1978.

Henry Moore: Sculptures et Dessins, introduction by Dominique Bozo. Editions des musées nationaux, Paris 1977.

Henry Moore: 80th Birthday Exhibition. Bradford Art Galleries and Museums, Bradford 1978.

Henry Moore at the Serpentine, text by David Sylvester. Arts Council of Great Britain, London 1978.

The Henry Moore Gift, introduction by John Russell. Tate Gallery, London 1978.

Henry Moore: Drawings 1969–79. Wildenstein, New York/Raymond Spencer Company, Much Hadham 1979.

Henry Moore: Maquetten, Bronzen, Handzeichnungen, text by Gerhard Bott. Eduard Roether Verlag, Darmstadt 1979.

Tapestry: Henry Moore & West Dean. Victoria and Albert Museum, London 1980.

Henry Moore: Sculture, Disegni, Opere Grafice, text by Andrea B. Del Guercio. Galleria Comunale d'Arte Moderna, Forte dei Marmi 1982.

Henry Moore. Samsung Foundation of Art and Culture, Seoul 1982.

Henry Moore: Head-Helmet. Durham Light Infantry Museum and Arts Centre, Durham 1982.

Henry Moore: Early Carvings 1920–1940, texts by Ann Garrould, Terry Friedman and David Mitchinson. City Art Galleries, Leeds 1982.

Henry Moore en Mexico: Escultura, Dibujo, Grafica de 1921 a 1987. Instituto Nacional de Bellas Artes-Cultura, Mexico City 1982.

Henry Moore, text by José María Salvador. Museo de Arte Contemporáneo, Caracas 1983.

Henry Moore: 60 Years of His Art, text by William S. Lieberman. The Metropolitan Museum of Art, New York; Thames and Hudson, London 1983.

Henry Moore: Skulpturen, Zeichnungen, Grafiken. Habarta Kunsthandel & Verlag, Vienna 1983.

Henry Moore: Shelter and Coal Mining Drawings, text by Julian Andrews. Ministerium für Kultur der Deutschen Demokratischen Republik, Berlin 1984.

Henry Moore: Mutter und Kind. Skulpturenmuseum Glaskasten, Marl 1984.

Henry Moore: The Reclining Figure, texts by Steven W. Rosen, David Mitchinson and Ann Garrould. Museum of Art, Columbus, Ohio 1984.

The Art of Henry Moore, text by David Mitchinson. Hong Kong Urban Council 1986.

The Art of Henry Moore, texts by David Mitchinson and William Packer. Metropolitan Art Museum, Tokyo; Art Museum, Fukuoka 1986.

Henry Moore: New Delhi 1987, edited by Ann Elliott and David Mitchinson, text by Norbert Lynton. National Gallery of Modern Art, New Delhi; British Council, London 1987.

Mother and Child: The Art of Henry Moore, edited by Gail Gelburd. Hofstra Museum and University, Hempstead, New York 1987.

Henry Moore, edited by Susan Compton. Royal Academy of Arts/Weidenfeld and Nicolson, London; Scribner's, New York 1988.

Henry Moore, edited by David Mitchinson. Fondation Pierre Gianadda, Martigny; Electa, Milan 1989.

PLATES

1 *Head of the Virgin*, 1922
  Marble, H 53.3 cm (21 in)
  The Henry Moore Foundation

2 *Figure*, 1923
  Verde di Prato, H 39.4 cm (15½ in)
  Erculiani Bauten Organization

3 *Head of a Girl*, 1923
  Terracotta, H 17.5 cm (6⅞ in)
  The Henry Moore Foundation

4 *Mother and Child*, 1924-5
  Hornton stone, H 63.5 cm (25 in)
  City Art Gallery, Manchester

3

4

2

5 *Two Heads*, 1924–5
   Mansfield stone, H 31.7 cm (12½ in)
   The Henry Moore Foundation

6, 7, 8 *Garden Reliefs*, 1926
    Portland stone, H 87.6 cm (34½ in)

6

7

8

9 *Half Figure*, 1929
Cast concrete, H 36.8 cm (15½ in)
The British Council, London

10 *Mask*, 1929
    Cast concrete, H 20 cm (8⅛ in)
    The Moore Danowski Trust

11 *Reclining Woman*, 1927
    Cast concrete, L 63.5 cm (25 in)
    The Moore Danowski Trust

10

11

12 *Seated Figure*, 1929
    Cast concrete, H 45.1 cm (17¾ in)
    The Henry Moore Foundation

13 *Reclining Figure*, 1929
    Alabaster, L 46.7 cm (18¾ in)

14 *Figure with Clasped Hands*, 1929
    Travertine marble, H 45.7 cm (18 in)
    Tel Aviv Museum

15 *Girl with Clasped Hands*, 1930
    Cumberland alabaster, H 41.5 cm (16½ in)
    The British Council, London

14

12

13

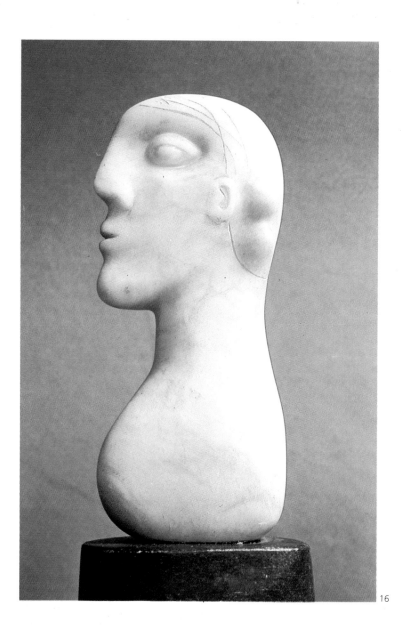

16

16 *Head*, 1930
Alabaster, H 20.3 cm (8 in)

17 *Composition*, 1931
Cumberland alabaster, L 41.5 cm (16⅜ in)
The Henry Moore Foundation

17

18 *Composition*, 1931
Green Hornton stone, H 48 cm (19 in)
The Moore Danowski Trust

19 *Reclining Figure*, 1930
    Ironstone, L 17.1 cm (6¾ in)
    Robert and Lisa Sainsbury Collection:
    University of East Anglia, Norwich

20 *Reclining Figure*, 1931, cast 1963
    Bronze, edition of 5, L 43.2 cm (17 in)

19

20

21 *Composition*, 1932
    African wood, H 38.8 cm (15¼ in)

22 *Girl*, 1931
    Ancaster stone, H 83.8 cm (33 in)
    The Trustees of the Tate Gallery, London

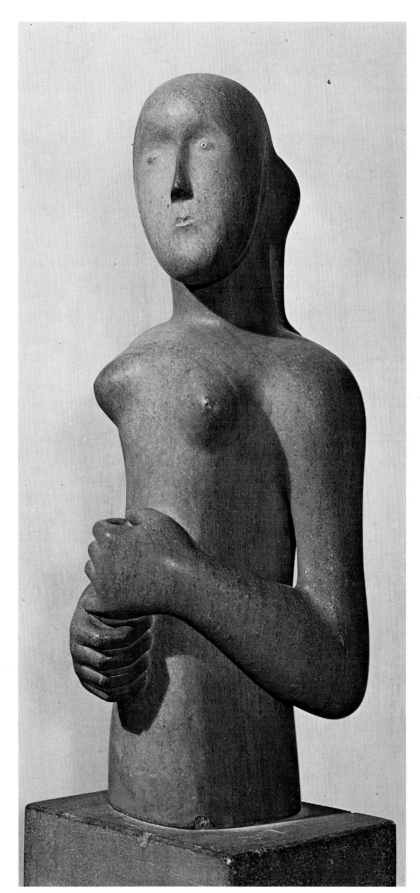

21

22

23 *Head*, 1932
Carved concrete, H 44.5 cm (17½ in)

25 *Figure*, 1933–4
Corsehill stone, H 77.5 cm (30 in)

26 *Composition*, 1933
Walnut wood, H 35.6 cm (14 in) approx.

27 *Hole and Lump*, 1934
Elmwood, H 68.6 cm (27 in)
The Henry Moore Foundation

28 *Figure*, 1932
Beechwood, H 36.2 cm (13 in)
Ernst Barlach Haus, Hamburg

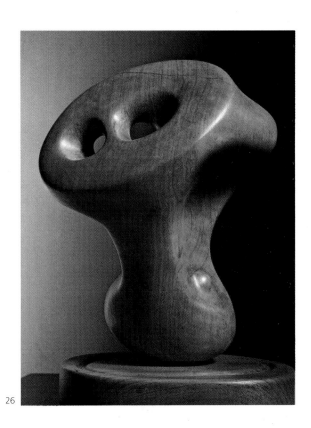

26

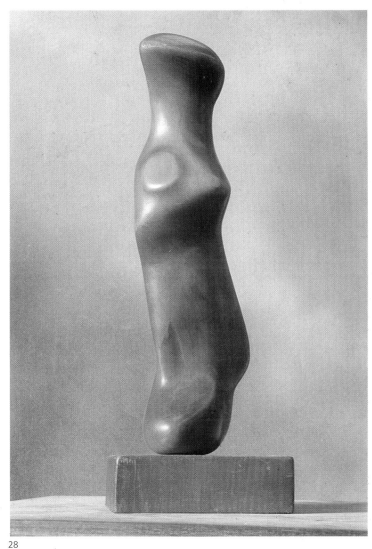

28

27

29

30

31

29 *Square Form*, 1934
    Burgundy stone, H 31.7 cm (12½ in)
    The Henry Moore Foundation

30 *Sculpture*, 1935
    White marble, L 55.9 cm (22 in)
    Art Institute of Chicago

31 *Four Forms*, 1936
    African wonderstone, L 55.9 cm (22 in)

32 *Two Forms*, 1936
    Hornton stone, H 1.05 m (41½ in)
    Philadelphia Museum of Art

33 *Four Piece Composition: Reclining Figure*, 1934
    Cumberland alabaster, L 50.8 cm (20 in)
    The Trustees of the Tate Gallery, London

32

33

34 *Mother and Child*, 1936
    Ancaster stone, H 45 cm (17¾ in)
    The British Council, London

35 *Reclining Figure*, 1936
Elmwood, L 1.06 m (42 in)
City Art Gallery, Wakefield

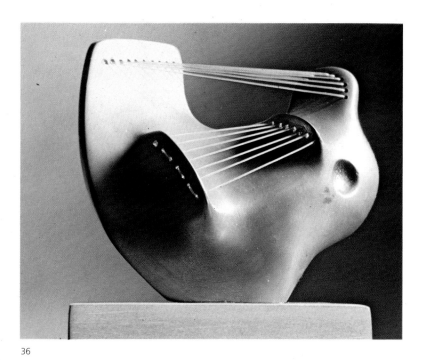

36

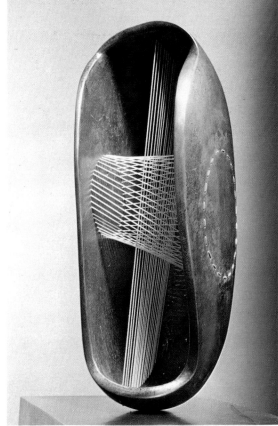

39

37

38

40

36 *Stringed Mother and Child*, 1938
Lead and string, L 12.1 cm (4¾ in)

37 *Stringed Figure*, 1939
Lead and string, L 21.6 cm (8¼ in)

38 *Stringed Reclining Figure*, 1939
Lead and string, L 25.4 cm (11¼ in)
University of Michigan, Ann Arbor

39 *Stringed Figure: Bowl*, 1938, cast 1967
Bronze and string, edition of 9, H 54.6 cm (21½ in)

40 *Stringed Head*, 1938
Bronze and string, edition of 5, H 7.7 cm (4⅜ in)

41 *Bird Basket*, 1939
Lignum vitae and string, L 41.9 cm (16½ in)

41

42 *Three Points*, 1939–40
    Cast iron, L 19 cm (7⅞ in)
    The Henry Moore Foundation

43 *Reclining Figure: One Arm*, 1938, cast 1969
    Bronze, edition of 9, L 30.5 cm (12 in)

44 *Reclining Figure: Snake*, 1939–40
    Bronze, edition of 9, L 28.9 cm (11⅜ in)

45 *Reclining Figure*, 1938
    Lead, L 33 cm (13 in)
    The Museum of Modern Art, New York

46 *Reclining Figure*, 1939
    Bronze, edition of 2, L 27.9 cm (11 in)

43

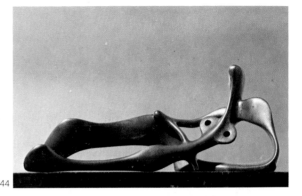

44

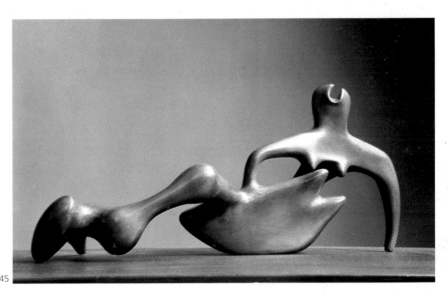

45

46

47 *Madonna and Child*, 1943
Terracotta, H 18.4 cm (7¼ in)

48 *Family Group*, 1944
Bronze, edition of 7, H 15.9 cm (6⅛ in)

49 *Family Group*, 1944
Bronze, edition of 8, H 15.5 cm (5½ in)

50 *Family Group*, 1945
Bronze, edition of 9, H 24.2 cm (9½ in)

51 *Family Group*, 1945
Bronze, edition of 7, H 18.1 cm (7⅛ in)

47

49

50

48

51

52 *Madonna and Child*, 1943–4
Hornton stone, H 1.50 m (59 in)
Church of St Matthew, Northampton

53 *Family Group*, 1948–9
    Bronze, edition of 4, H 1.52 m (60 in)

54 *Memorial Figure*, 1945–6
    Hornton stone, L 1.42 m (56 in)
    Dartington Hall, Totnes

55 *Three Standing Figures*, 1947–8
    Darley Dale stone, H 2.13 m (84 in)
    London Borough of Wandsworth, Battersea Park, London

56 *Rocking Chair No. 3*, 1950
    Bronze, edition of 6, H 31.7 cm (12½ in)

57 *Rocking Chair No. 2*, 1950
    Bronze, edition of 6, H 27.9 cm (11 in)

53

55

54

56

57

58 *Helmet Head No. 2*, 1950
   Lead, H 34.3 cm (13½ in)
   Staatsgalerie, Stuttgart

59 *Helmet Head and Shoulders*, 1952
    Bronze, edition of 10, H 16.5 cm (6¼ in)

60 *Animal Head*, 1951
    Bronze, edition of 8, L 30.5 cm (12 in)

61 *Maquette for Openwork Head and Shoulders*, 1950
    Bronze (unique), H 15.2 cm (6 in)

62 *Maquette for Strapwork Head*,
    1950, cast 1972
    Bronze, edition of 9, H 10.2 cm (4 in)

63 *Goat's Head*, 1952
    Bronze, edition of 10, H 20.3 cm (8 in)

59

61

62

60

63

64 *Reclining Figure: Festival*, 1951
    Plaster, L 2.28 m (90 in)
    The Trustees of the Tate Gallery, London

65 *Standing Figure*, 1950
    Fibreglass, H 2.18 m (86 in)
    The Henry Moore Foundation

64

66 *Three Standing Figures*, 1953
    Bronze, edition of 8, H 74.9 cm (29½ in)

67 *Mother and Child on Ladderback Chair*, 1952
    Bronze, edition of 7, H 40.6 cm (16 in)

68 *Leaf Figures 3 and 4*, 1952
    Bronze, edition of 11, H 49.5 cm (19½ in)

69 *Mother and Child*, 1953
    Bronze, edition of 8, H 50.8 cm (20 in)

66

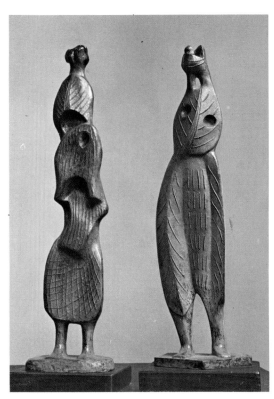

68

67

69

70 *Head of Draped Reclining Figure*, 1952–3
   Bronze (unique), H 28 cm (11 in)
   Private collection

71 *Draped Reclining Figure*, 1952–3
   Bronze, edition of 3, L 1.57 m (62 in)

70

71

72 *Reclining Figure: External Form*, 1953–4
    Bronze, edition of 6, L 2.20 m (86 in)

73 *Upright Internal/External Form*, 1952–3
    Bronze, edition of 3, H 2 m (79 in)

74, 75, 76 *King and Queen*, 1952–3
Bronze, edition of 5, H 1.64 m (64½ in)

74

75

76

79 *Animal Head*, 1956
    Bronze, edition of 10, L 55.9 cm (22 in)

80 *Bird*, 1955
    Bronze, edition of 12, L 14 cm (5½ in)

79

80

81 *Upright Motive No. 1: Glenkiln Cross*, 1955–6
Bronze, edition of 6, H 3.35 m (132 in)

82 *Upright Motive No. 8* (detail), 1955–6
Bronze, edition of 7, H 1.98 m (78 in)

83 *Upright Motive No. 5*, 1955–6
Bronze, edition of 7, H 2.13 m (84 in)

81

82

83

84 *Maquette for Fallen Warrior*, 1956
    Bronze, edition of 9, L 26.4 cm (10⅜ in)

85 *Falling Warrior*, 1956–7
    Bronze, edition of 10, L 1.5 m (59 in)

84

85

86 *Unesco Reclining Figure*, 1957–8
Roman travertine marble, L 5 m (200 in)
Unesco Headquarters, Paris

86

87 *Draped Seated Woman*, 1957–8
    Bronze, edition of 6, H 1.85 m (73 in)

87

88 *Three Motives against Wall No. 1*, 1958
    Bronze, edition of 12, L 1.06 m (42 in)

89 *Girl Seated against Square Wall*, 1958
    Bronze, edition of 12, H 1.01 m (40 in)

90 *Three Motives against Wall No. 2*, 1959
    Bronze, edition of 10, L 1.08 m (42¼ in)

91 *Two Seated Figures against Wall*, 1960
    Bronze, edition of 12, H 48.2 cm (19 in)

88

89

90

91

92 *Two Piece Reclining Figure No. 1*, 1959
    Bronze, edition of 6, L 1.93 m (76 in)

93 *Reclining Figure on Pedestal*, 1960
    Bronze, edition of 9, H 1.30 m (51¼ in)

94 *Three Part Object*, 1960
    Bronze, edition of 9, H 1.23 m (48½ in)

95 *Mother and Child: Arch*, 1959
    Bronze, edition of 6, L 49.5 cm (19½ in)

92

94

93

95

96 *Reclining Mother and Child*, 1960–61
Bronze, edition of 7, L 2.19 m (86½ in)

97 *Working Model for Standing Figure: Knife Edge*, 1961
Bronze, edition of 7, H 1.62 m (64 in)

98 *Three Piece Reclining Figure No. 1*, 1961–2
    Bronze, edition of 7, L 2.87 m (113 in)

99 *Large Slow Form*, 1962–8
    Bronze, edition of 9, L 77 cm (30¼ in)

100 *Three Piece Reclining Figure No. 2: Bridge Prop*, 1963
    Bronze, edition of 6, L 2.51 m (99 in)

98

99

100

101, 102, 103 *Locking Piece*, 1963–4
Bronze, edition of 3, H 2.92 m (114 in)

101

102

103

104, 105 *Working Model for Reclining Figure: Lincoln Center*, 1963–5
   Bronze, edition of 2, L 4.27 m (168 in)

104

105

Two Piece Reclining Figure No. 5, 1963–4
Bronze, edition of 3, L 3.72 m (147 in)

107 *The Arch*, 1963–9
Fibreglass, H 6 m (20 ft) approx.
The Henry Moore Foundation

108, 109 *Knife Edge Two Piece*, 1962–5
Bronze, edition of 3, L 3.65 m (144 in)

108

109

110 *Moon Head*, 1964
   Bronze, edition of 9, H 57 cm (22½ in)

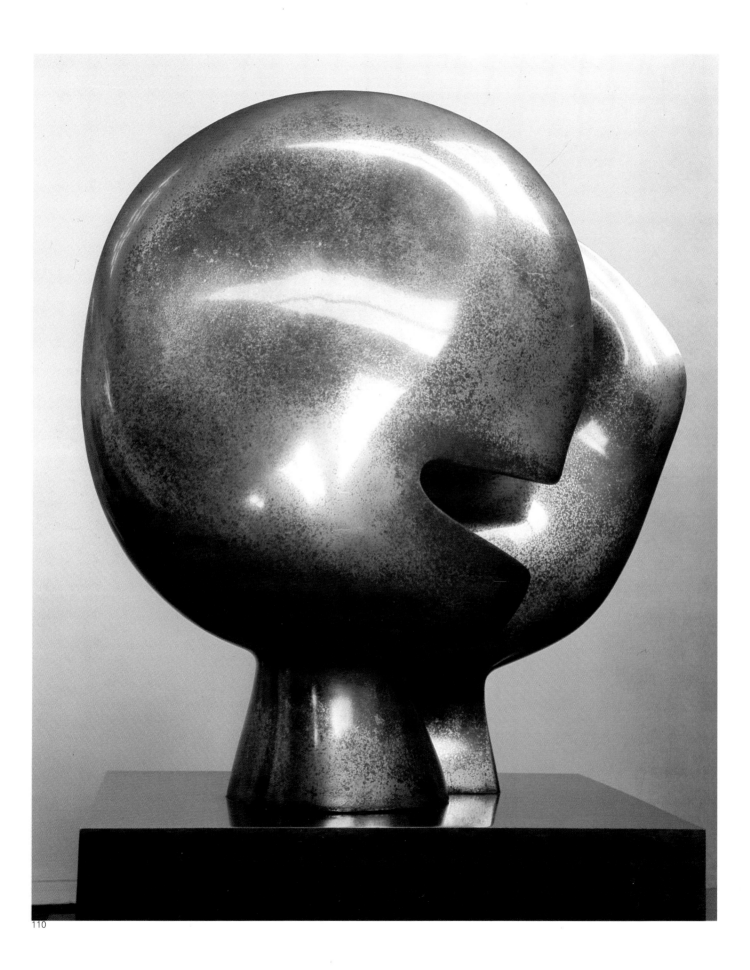

111 *Atom Piece*, 1964–5
   Bronze, edition of 6, H 1.19 m (47 in)

112 *Torso*, 1966
      White marble, H 79 cm (31 in)

113 *Two Forms*, 1964
      White marble, L 45.7 cm (18 in)

114 *Archer*, 1965
      White marble, H 80 cm (31½ in)
      Didrichsen Art Museum, Helsinki

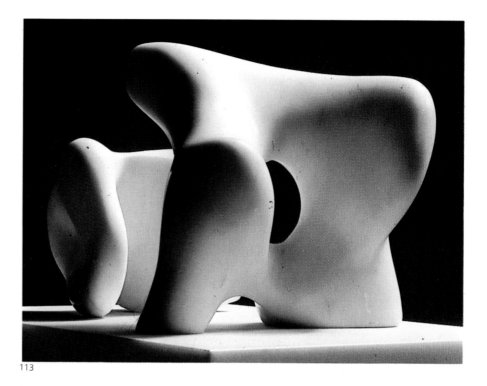

113

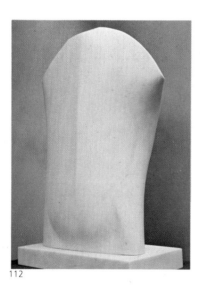

112

114

116 *Two Forms*, 1966
     Red travertine marble, L 1.52 m (60 in)

117 *Reclining Interior Oval*, 1965–8
     Red travertine marble, L 2.13 m (84 in)

116

117

118 *Three Rings*, 1966
   Rosa aurora marble, L 99.7 cm (39¼ in)

119 *Double Oval*, 1966
   Rosa aurora marble, L 96.5 cm (38 in) with base

120 *Three Rings*, 1966
   Red travertine marble, L 2.69 m (106 in)
   Ryda H. Levi Foundation, Lutherville, Maryland

118

119

120

121 *Large Two Forms*, 1966–9
Bronze, edition of 4, L 6.09 m (20 ft) approx.

122 *Two Piece Sculpture No. 7: Pipe*, 1966
      Bronze, edition of 9, L 94 cm (37 in)

123, 124 *Mother and Child*, 1967
    Rosa aurora marble, L 1.30 m (51¼ in)
    The Henry Moore Foundation

125 *Divided Oval: Butterfly*, 1967
    White marble, L 91.4 cm (36 in)

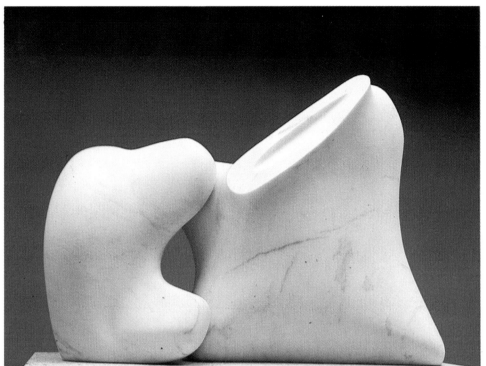

124

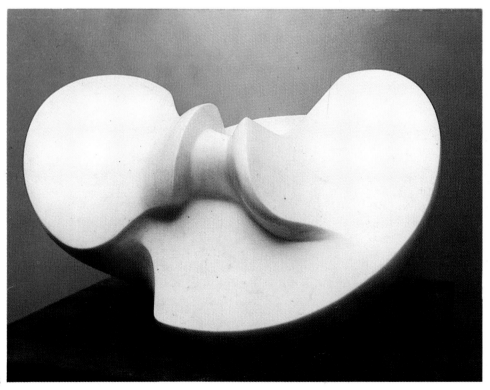

125

126

127

126 *Interlocking Two Piece Sculpture*, 1968–70
     White marble, L 3.25 m (128 in)
     The Hoffmann–La Roche Foundation, Basel

127 *Two Piece Carving: Interlocking*, 1968
     White marble, L 71.1 cm (28 in)

128 *Three Piece Sculpture: Vertebrae*, 1968–9
     Bronze, edition of 3, L 7.10 m (23 ft, 4 in) approx.

129

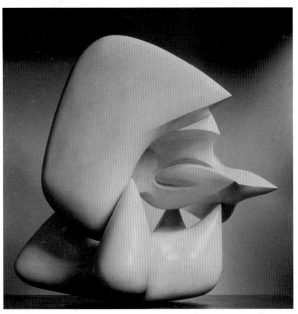

130

129 *Two Piece Sculpture No. 10: Interlocking*, 1968
     Bronze, edition of 7, L 91 cm (36 in)

130 *Two Piece Points: Skull*, 1969
     Fibreglass, edition of 4, H 76 cm (30 in)

131 *Pointed Torso*, 1969
     Bronze, edition of 12, H 66 cm (26 in)

132 *Architectural Project*, 1969
     Bronze, edition of 12, L 64 cm (25 in)

131   132

134 *Oval with Points*, 1968–70
     Bronze, edition of 6, H 3.27 m (130½ in)

135 *Square Form with Cut*, 1969
Black marble, L 1.40 m (55 in)
March Collection: Sa Torre Cega, Cala Ratjada, Mallorca

136 *Maquette for Square Form with Cut*, 1969–71
Plaster, H 16.5 cm (6½ in)
Art Gallery of Ontario, Toronto

135

137, 138 *Two Forms*, 1969
White marble, L 90.1 cm (35½ in)
City Art Gallery, Manchester

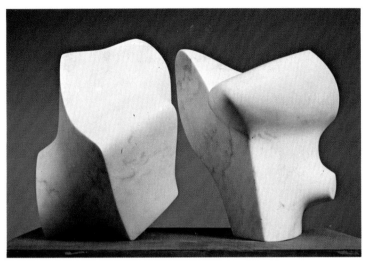

137

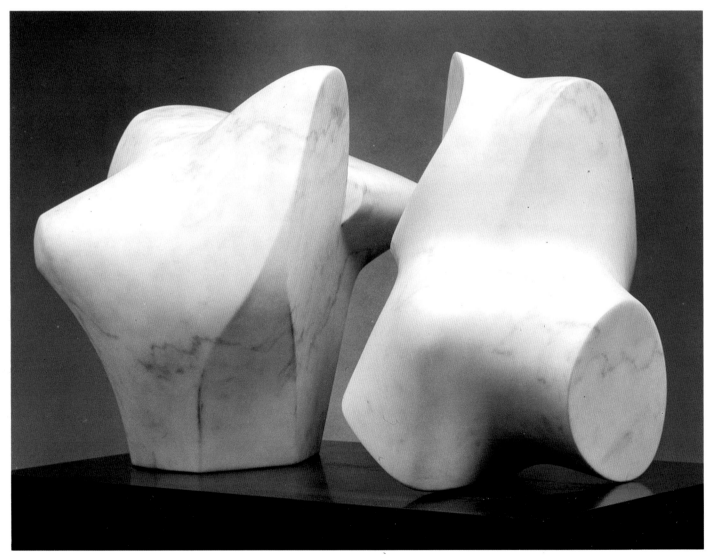

138

139 *Reclining Figure*, 1969–70
  Bronze, edition of 6, L 3.43 m (135 in)

140, 141 *Reclining Figure: Arch Leg,*
1969–70
Bronze, edition of 6, L 4.42 m (174 in)

140

141

142 *Animal Form*, 1969
   Travertine marble, L 1.22 m (48 in)

143 *Working Model for Animal Form*, 1969–71
   Bronze, edition of 9, L 66 cm (26 in)

144 *Oblong Composition*, 1970
   Red travertine marble, L 1.22 m (48 in)
   Kunsthalle, Karlsruhe

142

143

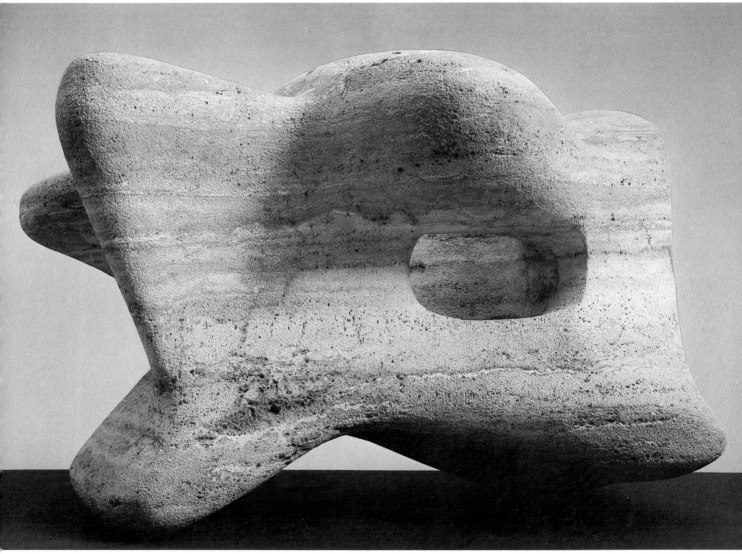

144

145 *Sheep Piece*, 1971–2
   Bronze, edition of 3, L 5.79 m (19 ft) approx.

146, 147 *Reclining Connected Forms*, 1969
Bronze, edition of 9, L 2.13 m (84 in)

146

147

148 *Large Four Piece Reclining Figure*, 1972–3
Bronze, edition of 7, L 4.02 m (158½ in)

149 *Working Model for Hill Arches*, 1972
Bronze, edition of 9, L 1.09 m (43 in)

150 *Hill Arches*, 1973
Bronze, edition of 3, L 5.5 m (18 ft) approx.

149

150

151

152

151, 152 *Reclining Mother and Child*, 1975–6
   Bronze, edition of 7, L 2.13 m (84 in)

153 *Goslar Warrior*, 1973–4
   Bronze, edition of 7, L 2.49 m (98 in)

153

154, 155 *Three Piece Reclining Figure:*
Draped, 1975
Bronze, edition of 7, L 4.47 m (14 ft, 8 in)

154

155

156 *Working Model for Reclining Figure: Angles*, 1975–7
Bronze, edition of 9, L 91.4 cm (36 in)

157 *Reclining Figure: Angles*, 1979
Bronze, edition of 9, L 2.18 m (86 in)

156

157

158 *Reclining Figure: Holes*, 1975–8
Elmwood, L 2.22 m (87½ in)
The Henry Moore Foundation

159 *Working Model for Reclining Figure: Prop*, 1976
   Bronze, edition of 9, L 80 cm (31½ in)

160 *Reclining Figure: Curved Smooth*, 1976
Bronze, edition of 9, L 21 cm (8¼ in)

161 *Reclining Figure: Thin*, 1976
Bronze, edition of 9, L 26 cm (10¼ in)

162 *Reclining Figure: Flint*, 1977
Bronze, edition of 9, L 21 cm (8¼ in)

160

161

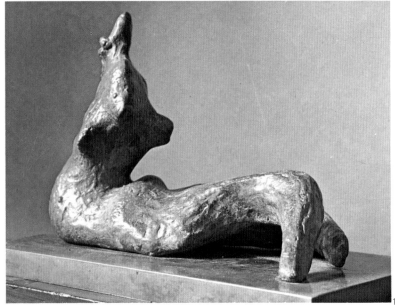

162

163 *Two Piece Reclining Figure: Thin*, 1976
Bronze, edition of 9, L 24.8 cm (9¾ in)

164 *Two Piece Reclining Figure: Double Circle*, 1976
Bronze, edition of 9, L 21.6 cm (8½ in)

165 *Reclining Figure: Single Leg*, 1976
Black granite, L 1.85 m (73 in)

163

164

165

166 *Reclining Figure: Bone Skirt*, 1978
Roman travertine marble, L 1.75 m (69 in)

166

167 *Draped Reclining Figure*, 1978
Roman travertine marble, L 1.83 m (72 in)
The Henry Moore Foundation

167

168

168 *Draped Mother and Child on Curved Bench*, 1980
Bronze, edition of 9, H 19 cm (7¹/₂ in)

169 *Thin Nude Mother and Child*, 1980
Bronze, edition of 9, H 17 cm (6⁵/₈ in)

170 *Draped Seated Mother and Child on Ground*, 1980
Bronze, edition of 9, L 20.3 cm (8 in)

169

170

171 *Mother and Child: Arms*, 1976–9
Bronze, edition of 9, L 79.7 cm (31½ in)

172 *Head*, 1976
     Black marble, H 38 cm (15 in) approx.

173 *Twin Heads*, 1976
     Bronze, edition of 9, L 15.9 cm (6¼ in)

174 *Butterfly*, 1977
     Marble, L 47 cm (18½ in)

175 *Mother and Child: Hands*, 1980
     Bronze, edition of 7, H 19.7 cm (7⅝ in)

176 *Three-Quarter Figure: Lines*, 1980
     Bronze, edition of 9, H 83.8 cm (33 in)

172

173

174

175

176

177, 178 *Two Piece Reclining Figure: Cut*, 1979–81
Bronze, edition of 3, L 4.7 m (15 ft, 5 in)

177

178

179 *Working Model for Reclining Woman: Elbow*, 1981
    Bronze, edition of 9, L 86.5 cm (34 in)

180 *Working Model for Draped Reclining Mother and Baby*, 1982
    Bronze, edition of 9, L 78.5 cm (31 in)

181 *Working Model for Mother and Child: Hood*, 1982
    Bronze, edition of 9, H 76 cm (30 in)

179

180

LIST OF PLATES

64 *Reclining Figure: Festival*, 1951
Plaster, L 2.28 m (90 in)
The Trustees of the Tate Gallery, London

65 *Standing Figure*, 1950
Fibreglass, H 2.18 m (86 in)
The Henry Moore Foundation

66 *Three Standing Figures*, 1953
Bronze, edition of 8, H 74.9 cm (29¹/₂ in)

67 *Mother and Child on Ladderback Chair*, 1952
Bronze, edition of 7, H 40.6 cm (16 in)

68 *Leaf Figures 3 and 4*, 1952
Bronze, edition of 11, H 49.5 cm (19¹/₂ in)

69 *Mother and Child*, 1953
Bronze, edition of 8, H 50.8 cm (20 in)

70 *Head of Draped Reclining Figure*, 1952–3
Bronze (unique), H 28 cm (11 in)
Private collection

71 *Draped Reclining Figure*, 1952–3
Bronze, edition of 3, L 1.57 m (62 in)

72 *Reclining Figure: External Form*, 1953–4
Bronze, edition of 6, L 2.20 m (86 in)

73 *Upright Internal/External Form*, 1952–3
Bronze, edition of 3, H 2 m (79 in)

74, 75, 76 *King and Queen*, 1952–3
Bronze, edition of 5, H 1.64 m (64¹/₂ in)

77 *Harlow Family Group*, 1954–5
Hadene stone, H 1.63 m (64¹/₂ in)
Harlow Art Trust, Harlow

78 *Warrior with Shield*, 1953–4
Bronze, edition of 6, H 1.55 m (60 in)

79 *Animal Head*, 1956
Bronze, edition of 10, L 55.9 cm (22 in)

80 *Bird*, 1955
Bronze, edition of 12, L 14 cm (5¹/₂ in)

81 *Upright Motive No. 1: Glenkiln Cross*, 1955–6
Bronze, edition of 6, H 3.35 m (132 in)

82 *Upright Motive No. 8* (detail), 1955–6
Bronze, edition of 7, H 1.98 m (78 in)

83 *Upright Motive No. 5*, 1955–6
Bronze, edition of 7, H 2.13 m (84 in)

84 *Maquette for Fallen Warrior*, 1956
Bronze, edition of 9, L 26.4 cm (10³/₈ in)

85 *Falling Warrior*, 1956–7
Bronze, edition of 10, L 1.5 m (59 in)

86 *Unesco Reclining Figure*, 1957–8
Roman travertine marble, L 5 m (200 in)
Unesco Headquarters, Paris

87 *Draped Seated Woman*, 1957–8
Bronze, edition of 6, H 1.85 m (73 in)

88 *Three Motives against Wall No. 1*, 1958
Bronze, edition of 12, L 1.06 m (42 in)

89 *Girl Seated against Square Wall*, 1958
Bronze, edition of 12, H 1.01 m (40 in)

90 *Three Motives against Wall No. 2*, 1959
Bronze, edition of 10, L 1.08 m (42¹/₄ in)

91 *Two Seated Figures against Wall*, 1960
Bronze, edition of 12, H 48.2 cm (19 in)

92 *Two Piece Reclining Figure No. 1*, 1959
Bronze, edition of 6, L 1.93 m (76 in)

93 *Reclining Figure on Pedestal*, 1960
Bronze, edition of 9, H 1.30 m (51¹/₄ in)

94 *Three Part Object*, 1960
Bronze, edition of 9, H 1.23 m (48¹/₂ in)

95 *Mother and Child: Arch*, 1959
Bronze, edition of 6, L 49.5 cm (19¹/₂ in)

96 *Reclining Mother and Child*, 1960–61
Bronze, edition of 7, L 2.19 m (86¹/₂ in)

97 *Working Model for Standing Figure: Knife Edge*, 1961
Bronze, edition of 7, H 1.62 m (64 in)

98 *Three Piece Reclining Figure No. 1*, 1961–2
Bronze, edition of 7, L 2.87 m (113 in)

99 *Large Slow Form*, 1962–8
Bronze, edition of 9, L 77 cm (30¹/₄ in)

100 *Three Piece Reclining Figure No. 2: Bridge Prop*, 1963
Bronze, edition of 6, L 2.51 m (99 in)

101, 102, 103 *Locking Piece*, 1963–4
Bronze, edition of 3, H 2.92 m (114 in)

104, 105 *Working Model for Reclining Figure: Lincoln Center*, 1963–5
Bronze, edition of 2, L 4.27 m (168 in)

106 *Two Piece Reclining Figure No. 5*, 1963–4
Bronze, edition of 3, L 3.72 m (147 in)

107 *The Arch*, 1963–9
Fibreglass, H 6 m (20 ft) approx.
The Henry Moore Foundation

108, 109 *Knife Edge Two Piece*, 1962–5
Bronze, edition of 3, L 3.65 m (144 in)

110 *Moon Head*, 1964
Bronze, edition of 9, H 57 cm (22¹/₂ in)

111 *Atom Piece*, 1964–5
Bronze, edition of 6, H 1.19 m (47 in)

112 *Torso*, 1966
White marble, H 79 cm (31 in)

113 *Two Forms*, 1964
White marble, L 45.7 cm (18 in)

114 *Archer*, 1965
White marble, H 80 cm (31¹/₂ in)
Didrichsen Art Museum, Helsinki

115 *Three Way Piece No. 2: Archer*, 1964–5
Bronze, edition of 2, L 3.4 m (134 in)

116 *Two Forms*, 1966
Red travertine marble, L 1.52 m (60 in)

117 *Reclining Interior Oval*, 1965–8
Red travertine marble, L 2.13 m (84 in)

118 *Three Rings*, 1966
Rosa aurora marble, L 99.7 cm (39¹/₄ in)

119 *Double Oval*, 1966
Rosa aurora marble, L 96.5 cm (38 in)
with base

120 *Three Rings*, 1966
Red travertine marble, L 2.69 m (106 in)
Ryda H. Levi Foundation, Lutherville, Maryland

121 *Large Two Forms*, 1966–9
Bronze, edition of 4,
L 6.09 m (20 ft) approx.

122 *Two Piece Sculpture No. 7: Pipe*, 1966
Bronze, edition of 9, L 94 cm (37 in)

123, 124 *Mother and Child*, 1967
Rosa aurora marble, L 1.30 m (51¹/₄ in)
The Henry Moore Foundation

125 *Divided Oval: Butterfly*, 1967
White marble, L 91.4 cm (36 in)

126 *Interlocking Two Piece Sculpture*, 1968–70
White marble, L 3.25 m (128 in)
The Hoffmann–La Roche Foundation, Basel

127 *Two Piece Carving: Interlocking*, 1968
White marble, L 71.1 cm (28 in)

128 *Three Piece Sculpture: Vertebrae*, 1968–9
Bronze, edition of 3,
L 7.10 m (23 ft, 4 in) approx.

129 *Two Piece Sculpture No. 10: Interlocking*, 1968
Bronze, edition of 7, L 91 cm (36 in)

130 *Two Piece Points: Skull*, 1969
Fibreglass, edition of 4, H 76 cm (30 in)

131 *Pointed Torso*, 1969
Bronze, edition of 12, H 66 cm (26 in)

132 *Architectural Project*, 1969
Bronze, edition of 12, L 64 cm (25 in)

133 *Large Spindle Piece*, 1968–74
Bronze, edition of 6, H 3.35 m (132 in)

134 *Oval with Points*, 1968–70
Bronze, edition of 6, H 3.27 m (130¹/₂ in)

135 *Square Form with Cut*, 1969
Black marble, L 1.40 m (55 in)
March Collection: Sa Torre Cega, Cala Ratjada, Mallorca

136 *Maquette for Square Form with Cut*, 1969–71
Plaster, H 16.5 cm (6½ in)
Art Gallery of Ontario, Toronto

137, 138 *Two Forms*, 1969
White marble, L 90.1 cm (35½ in)
City Art Gallery, Manchester

139 *Reclining Figure*, 1969–70
Bronze, edition of 6, L 3.43 m (135 in)

140, 141 *Reclining Figure: Arch Leg*, 1969–70
Bronze, edition of 6, L 4.42 m (174 in)

142 *Animal Form*, 1969
Travertine marble, L 1.22 m (48 in)

143 *Working Model for Animal Form*, 1969–71
Bronze, edition of 9, L 66 cm (26 in)

144 *Oblong Composition*, 1970
Red travertine marble, L 1.22 m (48 in)
Kunsthalle, Karlsruhe

145 *Sheep Piece*, 1971–2
Bronze, edition of 3, L 5.79 m (19 ft) approx.

146, 147 *Reclining Connected Forms*, 1969
Bronze, edition of 9, L 2.13 m (84 in)

148 *Large Four Piece Reclining Figure*, 1972–3
Bronze, edition of 7, L 4.02 m (158½ in)

149 *Working Model for Hill Arches*, 1972
Bronze, edition of 9, L 1.09 m (43 in)

150 *Hill Arches*, 1973
Bronze, edition of 3, L 5.5 m (18 ft) approx.

151, 152 *Reclining Mother and Child*, 1975–6
Bronze, edition of 7, L 2.13 m (84 in)

153 *Goslar Warrior*, 1973–4
Bronze, edition of 7, L 2.49 m (98 in)

154, 155 *Three Piece Reclining Figure: Draped*, 1975
Bronze, edition of 7, L 4.47 m (14 ft, 8 in)

156 *Working Model for Reclining Figure: Angles*, 1975–7
Bronze, edition of 9, L 91.4 cm (36 in)

157 *Reclining Figure: Angles*, 1979
Bronze, edition of 9, L 2.18 m (86 in)

158 *Reclining Figure: Holes*, 1975–8
Elmwood, L 2.22 m (87½ in)
The Henry Moore Foundation

159 *Working Model for Reclining Figure: Prop*, 1976
Bronze, edition of 9, L 80 cm (31½ in)

160 *Reclining Figure: Curved Smooth*, 1976
Bronze, edition of 9, L 21 cm (8¼ in)

161 *Reclining Figure: Thin*, 1976
Bronze, edition of 9, L 26 cm (10¼ in)

162 *Reclining Figure: Flint*, 1977
Bronze, edition of 9, L 21 cm (8¼ in)

163 *Two Piece Reclining Figure: Thin*, 1976
Bronze, edition of 9, L 24.8 cm (9¾ in)

164 *Two Piece Reclining Figure: Double Circle*, 1976
Bronze, edition of 9, L 21.6 cm (8½ in)

165 *Reclining Figure: Single Leg*, 1976
Black granite, L 1.85 m (73 in)

166 *Reclining Figure: Bone Skirt*, 1978
Roman travertine marble, L 1.75 m (69 in)

167 *Draped Reclining Figure*, 1978
Roman travertine marble, L 1.83 m (72 in)
The Henry Moore Foundation

168 *Draped Mother and Child on Curved Bench*, 1980
Bronze, edition of 9, H 19 cm (7½ in)

169 *Thin Nude Mother and Child*, 1980
Bronze, edition of 9, H 17 cm (6⅝ in)

170 *Draped Seated Mother and Child on Ground*, 1980
Bronze, edition of 9, L 20.3 cm (8 in)

171 *Mother and Child: Arms*, 1976–9
Bronze, edition of 9, L 79.7 cm (31½ in)

172 *Head*, 1976
Black marble, H 38 cm (15 in) approx.

173 *Twin Heads*, 1976
Bronze, edition of 9, L 15.9 cm (6¼ in)

174 *Butterfly*, 1977
Marble, L 47 cm (18½ in)

175 *Mother and Child: Hands*, 1980
Bronze, edition of 7, H 19.7 cm (7⅝ in)

176 *Three-Quarter Figure: Lines*, 1980
Bronze, edition of 9, H 83.8 cm (33 in)

177, 178 *Two Piece Reclining Figure: Cut*, 1979–81
Bronze, edition of 3, L 4.7 m (15 ft, 5 in)

179 *Working Model for Reclining Woman: Elbow*, 1981
Bronze, edition of 9, L 86.5 cm (34 in)

180 *Working Model for Draped Reclining Mother and Baby*, 1982
Bronze, edition of 9, L 78.5 cm (31 in)

181 *Working Model for Mother and Child: Hood*, 1982
Bronze, edition of 9, H 76 cm (30 in)